JAMESTOWN EDUCATION

Timed Readings Plus *in Science*

25 Two-Part Lessons
with Questions for
Building Reading Speed and Comprehension

BOOK 3

Glencoe McGraw-Hill

New York, New York   Columbus, Ohio   Chicago, Illinois   Peoria, Illinois   Woodland Hills, California

D1300505

JAMESTOWN  EDUCATION

Glencoe/McGraw-Hill

A Division of The **McGraw·Hill** *Companies*

ISBN: 0-07-827372-2

Copyright © The McGraw-Hill Companies, Inc. All rights reserved. Except as permitted under the United States Copyright Act of 1976, no part of this publication may be reproduced or distributed in any form or by any means, or stored in a database or retrieval system, without prior written permission of the publisher.

Send all queries to:
Glencoe/McGraw-Hill
8787 Orion Place
Columbus, OH 43240-4027

2 3 4 5 6 7 8 9 10 021 08 07 06 05 04 03 02

CONTENTS

To the Student

    Reading Faster and Better   2

    Mastering Reading Comprehension   3

    Working Through a Lesson   7

    Plotting Your Progress   8

To the Teacher

    About the Series   9

    Timed Reading and Comprehension   10

    Speed Versus Comprehension   10

    Getting Started   10

    Timing the Reading   11

    Teaching a Lesson   11

    Monitoring Progress   12

    Diagnosis and Evaluation   12

Lessons   13–112

Answer Key   114–115

Graphs   116–118

To the Student

You probably talk at an average rate of about 150 words a minute. If you are a reader of average ability, you read at a rate of about 250 words a minute. So your reading speed is nearly twice as fast as your speaking or listening speed. This example shows that reading is one of the fastest ways to get information.

The purpose of this book is to help you increase your reading rate and understand what you read. The 25 lessons in this book will also give you practice in reading science articles and in preparing for tests in which you must read and understand nonfiction passages within a certain time limit.

Reading Faster and Better

Following are some strategies that you can use to read the articles in each lesson.

Previewing

Previewing before you read is a very important step. This helps you to get an idea of what a selection is about and to recall any previous knowledge you have about the subject. Here are the steps to follow when previewing.

Read the title. Titles are designed not only to announce the subject but also to make the reader think. Ask yourself questions such as What can I learn from the title? What thoughts does it bring to mind?

What do I already know about this subject?

Read the first sentence. If they are short, read the first two sentences. The opening sentence is the writer's opportunity to get your attention. Some writers announce what they hope to tell you in the selection. Some writers state their purpose for writing; others just try to get your attention.

Read the last sentence. If it is short, read the final two sentences. The closing sentence is the writer's last chance to get ideas across to you. Some writers repeat the main idea once more. Some writers draw a conclusion—this is what they have been leading up to. Other writers summarize their thoughts; they tie all the facts together.

Skim the entire selection. Glance through the selection quickly to see what other information you can pick up. Look for anything that will help you read fluently and with under-standing. Are there names, dates, or numbers? If so, you may have to read more slowly.

Reading for Meaning

Here are some ways to make sure you are making sense of what you read.

Build your concentration. You cannot understand what you read if you are not concentrating. When you discover that your thoughts are straying, correct the situation right away. Avoid distractions and distracting situations. Keep in mind the information you learned from previewing. This will help focus your attention on the selection.

Read in thought groups. Try to see meaningful combinations of words—phrases, clauses, or sentences. If you look at only one word at a time (called word-by-word reading), both your comprehension and your reading speed suffer.

Ask yourself questions. To sustain the pace you have set for yourself and to maintain a high level of concentration and comprehension, ask yourself questions such as What does this mean? or How can I use this information? as you read.

Finding the Main Ideas

The paragraph is the basic unit of meaning. If you can quickly discover and understand the main idea of each paragraph, you will build your comprehension of the selection.

Find the topic sentence. The topic sentence, which contains the main idea, often is the first sentence of a paragraph. It is followed by sentences that support, develop, or explain the main idea. Sometimes a topic sentence comes at the end of a paragraph. When it does, the supporting details come first, building the base for the topic sentence. Some paragraphs do not have a topic sentence; all of the sentences combine to create a meaningful idea.

Understand paragraph structure. Every well-written paragraph has a purpose. The purpose may be to inform, define, explain or illustrate. The purpose should always relate to the main idea and expand on it. As you read each paragraph, see how the body of the paragraph tells you more about the main idea.

Relate ideas as you read. As you read the selection, notice how the writer puts together ideas. As you discover the relationship between the ideas, the main ideas come through quickly and clearly.

Mastering Reading Comprehension

Reading fast is not useful if you don't remember or understand what you read. The two exercises in Part A provide a check on how well you have understood the article.

Recalling Facts

These multiple-choice questions provide a quick check to see how well you recall important information from the article. As you learn to apply the reading strategies described earlier, you should be able to answer these questions more successfully.

Understanding Ideas

These questions require you to think about the main ideas in the article. Some main ideas are stated in the article; others are not. To answer some of the questions, you need to draw conclusions about what you read.

The five exercises in Part B require multiple answers. These exercises provide practice in applying comprehension and critical-thinking skills that you can use in all your reading.

Recognizing Words in Context

Always check to see whether the words around an unfamiliar word—its context—can give you a clue to the word's meaning. A word generally appears in a context related to its meaning.

Suppose, for example, that you are unsure of the meaning of the word *expired* in the following passage:

> Vera wanted to check out a book, but her library card had expired. She had to borrow my card, because she didn't have time to renew hers.

You could begin to figure out the meaning of *expired* by asking yourself a question such as, What could have happened to Vera's library card that would make her need to borrow someone else's card? You might realize that if Vera had to renew her card, its usefulness must have come to an end or run out. This would lead you to conclude that the word *expired* must mean "to come to an end" or "to run out." You would be right. The context suggested the meaning.

Context can also affect the meaning of a word you already know. The word *key*, for instance, has many meanings. There are musical keys, door keys, and keys to solving a mystery. The context in which the word *key* occurs will tell you which meaning is correct.

Sometimes a word is explained by the words that immediately follow it. The subject of a sentence and your knowledge about that subject might also help you determine the meaning of an unknown word. Try to decide the meaning of the word *revive* in the following sentence:

> Sunshine and water will revive those drooping plants.

The compound subject is *sunshine* and *water*. You know that plants need light and water to survive and that drooping plants are not healthy. You can figure out that *revive* means "to bring back to health."

Distinguishing Fact from Opinion

Every day you are called upon to sort out fact and opinion. Because much of what you read and hear contains both facts and opinions, you need to be able to tell the two apart.

Facts are statements that can be proved true. The proof must be objective and verifiable. You must be able to check for yourself to confirm a fact.

Look at the following facts. Notice that they can be checked for accuracy and confirmed. Suggested sources for verification appear in parentheses.

- Abraham Lincoln was the 16th president of the United States. (Consult biographies, social studies books, encyclopedias, and similar sources.)

- Earth revolves around the Sun. (Research in encyclopedias or astronomy books; ask knowledgeable people.)

- Dogs walk on four legs. (See for yourself.)

Opinions are statements that cannot be proved true. There is no objective evidence you can consult to check the truthfulness of an opinion. Unlike facts, opinions express personal beliefs or judgments. Opinions reveal how someone feels about a subject, not the facts about that subject. You might agree or disagree with someone's opinion, but you cannot prove it right or wrong.

Look at the following opinions. The reasons these statements are classified as opinions appear in parentheses.

- Abraham Lincoln was born to be a president. (You cannot prove this by referring to birth records. There is no evidence to support this belief.)

- Earth is the only planet in our solar system where intelligent life exists. (There is no proof of this. It may be proved true some day, but for now it is just an educated guess—not a fact.)

- The dog is a human's best friend. (This is not a fact; your best friend might not be a dog.)

As you read, be aware that facts and opinions are often mixed together. Both are useful to you as a reader. But to evaluate what you read and to read intelligently, you need to know the difference between the two.

Keeping Events in Order

Sequence, or chronological order, is the order of events in a story or article or the order of steps in a process. Paying attention to the sequence of events or steps will help you follow what is happening, predict what might happen next, and make sense of a passage.

To make the sequence as clear as possible, writers often use signal words to help the reader get a more exact idea of when things happen. Following is a list of frequently used signal words and phrases:

until	first
next	then
before	after
finally	later
when	while
during	now
at the end	by the time
as soon as	in the beginning

Signal words and phrases are also useful when a writer chooses to relate details or events out of sequence. You need to pay careful attention to determine the correct chronological order.

Making Correct Inferences

Much of what you read *suggests* more than it *says*. Writers often do not state ideas directly in a text. They can't. Think of the time and space it would take to state every idea. And think of how boring that would be! Instead, writers leave it to you, the reader, to fill in the information they leave out—to make inferences. You do this by combining clues in the

5

story or article with knowledge from your own experience.

You make many inferences every day. Suppose, for example, that you are visiting a friend's house for the first time. You see a bag of kitty litter. You infer (make an inference) that the family has a cat. Another day you overhear a conversation. You catch the names of two actors and the words *scene, dialogue,* and *directing.* You infer that the people are discussing a movie or play.

In these situations and others like them, you infer unstated information from what you observe or read. Readers must make inferences in order to understand text.

Be careful about the inferences you make. One set of facts may suggest several inferences. Some of these inferences could be faulty. A correct inference must be supported by evidence.

Remember that bag of kitty litter that caused you to infer that your friend has a cat? That could be a faulty inference. Perhaps your friend's family uses the kitty litter on their icy sidewalks to create traction. To be sure your inference is correct, you need more evidence.

Understanding Main Ideas

The main idea is the most important idea in a paragraph or passage—the idea that provides purpose and direction. The rest of the selection explains, develops, or supports the main idea. Without a main idea, there would be only a collection of unconnected thoughts.

In the following paragraph, the main idea is printed in italics. As you read, observe how the other sentences develop or explain the main idea.

Typhoon Chris hit with full fury today on the central coast of Japan. Heavy rain from the storm flooded the area. High waves carried many homes into the sea. People now fear that the heavy rains will cause mudslides in the central part of the country. The number of people killed by the storm may climb past the 200 mark by Saturday.

In this paragraph, the main-idea statement appears first. It is followed by sentences that explain, support, or give details. Sometimes the main idea appears at the end of a paragraph. Writers often put the main idea at the end of a paragraph when their purpose is to persuade or convince. Readers may be more open to a new idea if the reasons for it are presented first.

As you read the following paragraph, think about the overall impact of the supporting ideas. Their purpose is to convince the reader that the main idea in the last sentence should be accepted.

Last week there was a head-on collision at Huntington and Canton streets. Just a month ago a pedestrian was struck there. Fortunately, she was only slightly injured. In the past year, there have been more accidents there than at any other corner in the city. In fact, nearly 10 percent of all accidents in the city occur at the corner. This intersection is very dangerous, and a traffic signal should be installed there before a life is lost.

The details in the paragraph progress from least important to most important. They achieve their full effect in the main idea statement at the end.

In many cases, the main idea is not expressed in a single sentence. The reader is called upon to interpret all of the ideas expressed in the paragraph and to decide upon a main idea. Read the following paragraph.

The American author Jack London was once a pupil at the Cole Grammar School in Oakland, California. Each morning the class sang a song. When the teacher noticed that Jack wouldn't sing, she sent him to the principal. He returned to class with a note. The note said that Jack could be excused from singing with the class if he would write an essay every morning.

In this paragraph, the reader has to interpret the individual ideas and to decide on a main idea. This main idea seems reasonable: Jack London's career as a writer began with a punishment in grammar school.

Understanding the concept of the main idea and knowing how to find it is important. Transferring that understanding to your reading and study is also important.

Working Through a Lesson

Part A

1. **Preview the article.** Locate the timed selection in Part A of the lesson that you are going to read. Wait for your teacher's signal to preview. You will have 20 seconds for previewing. Follow the previewing steps described on page 2.

2. **Read the article.** When your teacher gives you the signal, begin reading. Read carefully so that you will be able to answer questions about what you have read. When you finish reading, look at the board and note your reading time. Write this time at the bottom of the page on the line labeled Reading Time.

3. **Complete the exercises.** Answer the 10 questions that follow the article. There are 5 fact questions and 5 idea questions. Choose the best answer to each question and put an X in that box.

4. **Correct your work.** Use the Answer Key at the back of the book to check your answers. Circle any wrong answer and put an X in the box you should have marked. Record the number of correct answers on the appropriate line at the end of the lesson.

Part B

1. **Preview and read the passage.** Use the same techniques you

used to read Part A. Think about what you are reading.

2. **Complete the exercises.** Instructions are given for answering each category of question. There are 15 responses for you to record.

3. **Correct your work.** Use the Answer Key at the back of the book. Circle any wrong answer and write the correct letter or number next to it. Record the number of correct answers on the appropriate line at the end of the lesson.

Plotting Your Progress

1. **Find your reading rate.** Turn to the Reading Rate graph on page 116. Put an X at the point where the vertical line that represents the lesson intersects your reading time, shown along the left-hand side. The right-hand side of the graph will reveal your words-per-minute reading speed.

2. **Find your comprehension score.** Add your scores for Part A and Part B to determine your total number of correct answers. Turn to the Comprehension Score graph on page 117. Put an X at the point where the vertical line that represents your lesson intersects your total correct answers, shown along the left-hand side. The right-hand side of the graph will show the percentage of questions you answered correctly.

3. **Complete the Comprehension Skills Profile.** Turn to page 118. Record your incorrect answers for the Part B exercises. The five Part B skills are listed along the bottom. There are five columns of boxes, one column for each question. For every incorrect answer, put an X in a box for that skill.

To get the most benefit from these lessons, you need to take charge of your own progress in improving your reading speed and comprehension. Studying these graphs will help you to see whether your reading rate is increasing and to determine what skills you need to work on. Your teacher will also review the graphs to check your progress.

TO THE TEACHER

About the Series

Timed Readings Plus in Science includes 10 books at reading levels 4–13, with one book at each level. Book One contains material at a fourth-grade reading level; Book Two at a fifth-grade level, and so on. The readability level is determined by the Fry Readability Scale and is not to be confused with grade or age level. The books are designed for use with students at middle-school level and above.

The purposes of the series are as follows:

- to provide systematic, structured reading practice that helps students improve their reading rate and comprehension skills

- to give students practice in reading and understanding informational articles in the content area of science

- to give students experience in reading various text types—informational, expository, narrative, and prescriptive

- to prepare students for taking standardized tests that include timed reading passages in various content areas

- to provide materials with a wide range of reading levels so that students can continue to practice and improve their reading rate and comprehension skills

Because the books are designed for use with students at designated reading levels rather than in a particular grade, the science topics in this series are not correlated to any grade-level curriculum. Most standardized tests require students to read and comprehend science passages. This series provides an opportunity for students to become familiar with the particular requirements of reading science. For example, the vocabulary in a science article is important. Students need to know certain words in order to understand the concepts and the information.

Each book in the series contains 25 two-part lessons. Part A focuses on improving reading rate. This section of the lesson consists of a 400-word timed informational article on a science topic followed by two multiple-choice exercises. Recalling Facts includes five fact questions; Understanding Ideas includes five critical-thinking questions.

Part B concentrates on building mastery in critical areas of comprehension. This section consists of a nontimed passage—the "plus" passage—followed by five exercises that address five major comprehension skills. The passage varies in length; its subject matter relates to the content of the timed selection.

Timed Reading and Comprehension

Timed reading is the best-known method of improving reading speed. There is no point in someone's reading at an accelerated speed if the person does not understand what she or he is reading. Nothing is more important than comprehension in reading. The main purpose of reading is to gain knowledge and insight, to understand the information that the writer and the text are communicating.

Few students will be able to read a passage once and answer all of the questions correctly. A score of 70 or 80 percent correct is normal. If the student gets 90 or 100 percent correct, he or she is either reading too slowly or the material is at too low a reading level. A comprehension or critical thinking score of less than 70 percent indicates a need for improvement.

One method of improving comprehension and critical-thinking skills is for the student to go back and study each incorrect answer. First, the student should reread the question carefully. It is surprising how many students get the wrong answer simply because they have not read the question carefully. Then the student should look back in the passage to find the place where the question is answered, reread that part of the passage, and think about how to arrive at the correct answer. It is important to be able to recognize a correct answer when it is embedded in the text. Teacher guidance or class discussion will help the student find an answer.

Speed Versus Comprehension

It is not unusual for comprehension scores to decline as reading rate increases during the early weeks of timed readings. If this happens, students should attempt to level off their speed—but not lower it—and concentrate more on comprehension. Usually, if students maintain the higher speed and concentrate on comprehension, scores will gradually improve and within a week or two be back up to normal levels of 70 to 80 percent.

It is important to achieve a proper balance between speed and comprehension. An inefficient reader typically reads everything at one speed, usually slowly. Some poor readers, however, read rapidly but without satisfactory comprehension. It is important to achieve a balance between speed and comprehension. The practice that this series provides enables students to increase their reading speed while maintaining normal levels of comprehension.

Getting Started

As a rule, the passages in a book designed to improve reading speed should be relatively easy. The student should not have much difficulty with the vocabulary or the subject matter. Don't worry about the passages being too easy; students should see how quickly and efficiently they can read a passage.

Begin by assigning students to a level. A student should start with a book that is one level below his or her current reading level. If a student's reading level is not known, a suitable starting point would be one or two levels below the student's present grade in school.

Introduce students to the contents and format of the book they are using. Examine the book to see how it is organized. Talk about the parts of each lesson. Discuss the purpose of timed reading and the use of the progress graphs at the back of the book.

Timing the Reading

One suggestion for timing the reading is to have all students begin reading the selection at the same time. After one minute, write on the board the time that has elapsed and begin updating it at 10-second intervals (1:00, 1:10, 1:20, etc.). Another option is to have individual students time themselves with a stopwatch.

Teaching a Lesson

Part A

1. Give students the signal to begin previewing the lesson. Allow 20 seconds, then discuss special science terms or vocabulary that students found.

2. Use one of the methods described above to time students as they read the passage. (Include the 20-second preview time as part of the first minute.) Tell students to write down the last time shown on the board or the stopwatch when they finish reading. Have them record the time in the designated space after the passage.

3. Next, have students complete the exercises in Part A. Work with them to check their answers, using the Answer Key that begins on page 114. Have them circle incorrect answers, mark the correct answers, and then record the numbers of correct answers for Part A on the appropriate line at the end of the lesson. Correct responses to eight or more questions indicate satisfactory comprehension and recall.

Part B

1. Have students read the Part B passage and complete the exercises that follow it. Directions are provided with each exercise. Correct responses require deliberation and discrimination.

2. Work with students to check their answers. Then discuss the answers with them and have them record the number of correct answers for Part B at the end of the lesson.

Have students study the correct answers to the questions they answered incorrectly. It is important that they understand why a particular answer is correct or incorrect.

Have them reread relevant parts of a passage to clarify an answer. An effective cooperative activity is to have students work in pairs to discuss their answers, explain why they chose the answers they did, and try to resolve differences.

Monitoring Progress

Have students find their total correct answers for the lesson and record their reading time and scores on the graphs on pages 116 and 117. Then have them complete the Comprehension Skills Profile on page 118. For each incorrect response to a question in Part B, students should mark an X in the box above each question type.

The legend on the Reading Rate graph automatically converts reading times to words-per-minute rates. The Comprehension Score graph automatically converts the raw scores to percentages.

These graphs provide a visual record of a student's progress. This record gives the student and you an opportunity to evaluate the student's progress and to determine the types of exercises and skills he or she needs to concentrate on.

Diagnosis and Evaluation

The following are typical reading rates.

Slow Reader—150 Words Per Minute

Average Reader—250 Words Per Minute

Fast Reader—350 Words Per Minute

A student who consistently reads at an average or above-average rate (with satisfactory comprehension) is ready to advance to the next book in the series.

A column of Xs in the Comprehension Skills Profile indicates a specific comprehension weakness. Using the profile, you can assess trends in student performance and suggest remedial work if necessary.

Our Solar System

A solar system consists of a star, its orbiting planets, and all other material that is held in by the gravity of the star. Our solar system is made up of the Sun, the planets, and millions of smaller objects, such as asteroids, comets, and meteoroids. Our solar system is one of many solar systems in the universe. Astronomers so far have found at least 50 other solar systems.

The Sun is made up entirely of gases. Hydrogen gas in the core of the Sun undergoes fusion to form helium gas. This process gives off energy in the form of heat and light. It is so powerful that the core of the Sun has a temperature of about 15 million degrees Celsius (27 million degrees Fahrenheit). All life on Earth depends on the heat and light of the Sun.

Of the planets in our solar system, Mercury, Venus, Earth, and Mars are closest to the Sun. They are rocky planets that are surrounded by a large asteroid belt. Jupiter, Saturn, Uranus, and Neptune are farther away from the Sun. They have a liquid surface and a thick, outer layer of gas. Thin rings of dust, rock, and ice surround each of the outer planets. All of these planets except Mercury and Venus have at least one moon.

Pluto is the planet farthest from the Sun. Pluto is a tiny, solid planet with an odd orbit. The path it makes around the Sun is not like the paths of the other planets. Most astronomers do not consider Pluto to be a major planet.

Many smaller objects orbit the Sun. Asteroids are the largest of these objects. Most asteroids are found in the asteroid belt between Mars and Jupiter. The largest known asteroid, Ceres, is about 1,000 kilometers (600 miles) across.

Comets are made of ice and rock. Comets come from the coldest parts of our solar system. Objects in this region are propelled into new orbits from time to time. As a comet nears the Sun, the ice in its core turns to gas. It leaves a tail of glowing dust.

The other objects in our solar system break off from asteroids, comets, planets, and moons. These broken chunks of rock and metal are meteoroids. Sometimes one of these space rocks lands on Earth and serves as a reminder that there are other bodies in our solar system.

Reading Time _____

Recalling Facts

1. Jupiter is a
   - ❏ a. rocky planet.
   - ❏ b. planet with a liquid surface.
   - ❏ c. moon.

2. The star at the center of our solar system is
   - ❏ a. Ceres.
   - ❏ b. Pluto.
   - ❏ c. the Sun.

3. Meteoroids are
   - ❏ a. liquid planets.
   - ❏ b. chunks of rock and metal.
   - ❏ c. stars.

4. A solid planet with an odd orbit around the Sun is
   - ❏ a. Pluto.
   - ❏ b. Uranus.
   - ❏ c. Neptune.

5. Planets, other orbiting material, and the star they move around form
   - ❏ a. helium gas.
   - ❏ b. a comet.
   - ❏ c. a solar system.

Understanding Ideas

6. Pluto is not grouped with the other planets because it is
   - ❏ a. close to the Sun.
   - ❏ b. very different from the other planets.
   - ❏ c. a star.

7. You can infer that planets exist
   - ❏ a. outside our solar system.
   - ❏ b. only in our solar system.
   - ❏ c. only within the asteroid belt.

8. At the very center of a solar system is a
   - ❏ a. planet.
   - ❏ b. comet.
   - ❏ c. star.

9. You can conclude that all large and small bodies in a solar system orbit
   - ❏ a. a star.
   - ❏ b. a moon.
   - ❏ c. the largest planet.

10. As a comet moves away from the Sun,
    - ❏ a. it leaves the solar system.
    - ❏ b. it collides with a planet.
    - ❏ c. gas changes back to ice.

In our solar system, Mars is the planet that is most like Earth. A day on Mars is just over 24 hours long. There are seasons on Mars just as there are on Earth. Even some of the land features are similar. Both Mars and Earth have canyons, volcanoes, deserts, and polar ice caps.

Scientists once believed there was life on Mars. Dark markings on the surface of Mars appeared to change shape over time. Scientists believed the marks could be plant life. Other marks looked like canals. Some people believed intelligent life forms had built canals to carry water from the poles to the deserts. Further study revealed, however, that none of the marks were plants or canals.

Most scientists today agree that Mars cannot support life. Mars has in fact a very harsh environment. The air on Mars is very thin and made up mostly of carbon dioxide. It does not trap heat the way Earth's oxygen-rich atmosphere does. The temperature on Mars can reach 27°C (81°F) during the day in some areas, but it can drop to a frigid –143°C (–225°F) at the polar ice caps. In these conditions, liquid water is unlikely to be present on the surface of Mars.

A meteorite that appears to have come from Mars provides evidence that there were primitive bacteria there billions of years ago. Scientists are continuing to investigate this possibility.

1. Recognizing Words in Context

Find the word *frigid* in the passage. One definition below is closest to the meaning of that word. One definition has the opposite or nearly opposite meaning. The remaining definition has a completely different meaning. Label the definitions C for *closest,* O for *opposite or nearly opposite,* and D for *different.*

_____ a. negative

_____ b. cold

_____ c. scorching

2. Distinguishing Fact from Opinion

Two of the statements below present *facts,* which can be proved correct. The other statement is an *opinion,* which expresses someone's thoughts or beliefs. Label the statements F for *fact* and O for *opinion.*

_____ a. Scientists understand Mars better now than they did before.

_____ b. People who think intelligent beings once lived on Mars are foolish.

_____ c. Mars is colder than Earth.

3. Keeping Events in Order

Two of the statements below describe events that happened at the same time. The other statement describes an event that happened before or after those events. Label them S for *same time*, B for *before*, and A for *after*.

_____ a. Dark markings on Mars were thought to be plant growth.

_____ b. Scientists found that Mars has too harsh an environment to support life.

_____ c. Some marks on the surface of Mars were thought to be canals built by Martians.

4. Making Correct Inferences

Two of the statements below are correct *inferences,* or reasonable guesses. They are based on information in the passage. The other statement is an incorrect, or faulty, inference. Label the statements C for *correct* inference and F for *faulty* inference.

_____ a. Future space missions to Mars will search for evidence that bacteria once lived there.

_____ b. Humans could not survive on Mars without special equipment.

_____ c. The air and temperature on Mars make it completely different from Earth.

5. Understanding Main Ideas

One of the statements below expresses the main idea of the passage. One statement is too general, or too broad. The other explains only part of the passage; it is too narrow. Label the statements M for *main idea*, B for *too broad*, and N for *too narrow*.

_____ a. Life may exist on other planets in the universe.

_____ b. Although Mars is similar to Earth, it cannot support life.

_____ c. Mars has an atmosphere very different from that of Earth.

Correct Answers, Part A _____

Correct Answers, Part B _____

Total Correct Answers _____

The human eye works together with the brain to provide our sense of sight. Light rays bouncing off objects travel through the eye. The eyes collect light and send signals to the brain, which create visual images.

The eye is a round organ filled with clear fluid. When light travels into the eye, it first passes through the cornea. This clear layer on the outside of the eyeball helps to protect the eye from harm, and it helps to focus light deep into the eye.

Next, light travels through the pupil. The pupil is a black spot that controls the amount of light that enters the eye. Surrounding the pupil is the round, colorful iris. The muscles of the iris relax to open the pupil to let light in when it is dim. When it is very bright, the iris tightens to make the pupil smaller. Less light enters the eye when the pupil is smaller.

From the pupil, light travels through a clear disk called a lens. The lens focuses light and can change shape to focus on objects at different distances. The lens bulges to focus on nearby objects and flattens out to focus on faraway objects.

Focused light from the lens hits the retina, which lines the back of the eyeball. The retina is made up of nerve cells called rods and cones. The rods are responsible for black-and-white vision in very dim light. The cones are responsible for color vision in brighter light. When a person enters a dark room after being in bright light, the eyes adjust. The pupil widens to collect as much light as possible to be able to see in the dark. But changes in the pupil are not enough to adjust to extreme changes of light. The retina plays an important role. A pigment in the rods makes vision in darkness possible. Bright light bleaches this pigment and prevents it from working. It takes time for the pigment to be restored so that the eyes can see in the dark.

As light hits the rods and cones, the retina sends messages to the brain along the optic nerve. Different parts of the brain work together to make sense of the messages from the eyes, and finally an image is formed. With messages from both eyes, the brain can judge the distance, size, movement, and speed of the objects in sight.

Reading Time _____

Recalling Facts

1. The retina is made up of
   - ❏ a. cones and rods.
   - ❏ b. lenses.
   - ❏ c. clear fluid.

2. The eye is a
   - ❏ a. solid ball.
   - ❏ b. ball filled with fluid.
   - ❏ c. thin disk.

3. Messages are sent to the brain along
   - ❏ a. blood vessels.
   - ❏ b. nerves.
   - ❏ c. bones.

4. The part of the eye that can change shape to focus on objects at different distances is the
   - ❏ a. pupil.
   - ❏ b. retina.
   - ❏ c. lens.

5. The parts of the body that provide our sense of sight are the eyes and
   - ❏ a. the brain.
   - ❏ b. the ears.
   - ❏ c. the rest of the face.

Understanding Ideas

6. Light travels through the cornea and lens before it
   - ❏ a. passes through the pupil.
   - ❏ b. reaches the eye.
   - ❏ c. hits the retina.

7. It is possible to conclude from the article that sight would be impossible without
   - ❏ a. cones.
   - ❏ b. light.
   - ❏ c. pigment.

8. The parts of the eye that adjust to extreme changes of light are
   - ❏ a. the pupil and the retina.
   - ❏ b. the cornea and optic nerve.
   - ❏ c. the lens and the nerve cells.

9. It is likely that in bright sunlight, the pupil
   - ❏ a. shuts to keep out all light.
   - ❏ b. closes a bit to keep out some light.
   - ❏ c. opens to let all the light in.

10. It is possible to conclude from the article that the signals sent to the brain by the optic nerve are
    - ❏ a. the result of changes in the liquid that fills the eye.
    - ❏ b. sent by the lens and the cornea.
    - ❏ c. based on the pattern of light that hits the retina.

Many people have imperfect vision. Vision problems can result from genetic factors or from diseases. Some people are unable to see nearby objects clearly. Others cannot see distant objects clearly. Eye problems often increase as people get older. Doctors correct vision through the use of eyeglasses, contact lenses, or surgery.

People first wore glasses in Europe in the 1200s. Before that, they used handheld lenses to see better when reading, but there were no lenses for seeing things at a distance. Benjamin Franklin made bifocal glasses in the 1700s. Each lens has two parts, one to help with near vision and one for distance vision. In 1938, Katherine Blodgett created a coating for glass to reduce glare. Modern glasses are better than ever.

Contact lenses are worn directly on the eye. Leonardo da Vinci drew plans for the first contact lenses. In the late 1800s, A. Eugen Fick and Edouard Kalt made contact lenses out of glass. Today there are many types of contact lenses. They can be hard or soft, extended wear or disposable.

Eye surgery is not a new treatment for poor sight. Records show that eye surgery was done in ancient times. Today, surgery can treat eye diseases that cause blindness. Lasers are often used in eye surgery.

1. **Recognizing Words in Context**

   Find the word *genetic* in the passage. One definition below is closest to the meaning of that word. One definition has the opposite or nearly opposite meaning. The remaining definition has a completely different meaning. Label the definitions C for *closest,* O for *opposite or nearly opposite,* and D for *different.*

   _____ a. caused by the environment

   _____ b. inherited

   _____ c. exposed

2. **Distinguishing Fact from Opinion**

   Two of the statements below present *facts,* which can be proved correct. The other statement is an *opinion,* which expresses someone's thoughts or beliefs. Label the statements F for *fact* and O for *opinion.*

   _____ a. It is easier to read with glasses than with a hand-held lens.

   _____ b. Benjamin Franklin made bifocal glasses.

   _____ c. Eye surgery was done in ancient times.

3. **Keeping Events in Order**

Label the statements below 1, 2, and 3 to show the order in which the events happened.

_____ a. Bifocals were invented.

_____ b. Katherine Blodgett invented a coating that reduces glare on glass.

_____ c. Only handheld lenses were available to improve vision.

4. **Making Correct Inferences**

Two of the statements below are correct *inferences,* or reasonable guesses. They are based on information in the passage. The other statement is an incorrect, or faulty, inference. Label the statements C for *correct* inference and F for *faulty* inference.

_____ a. Today, any eye problem can be fixed.

_____ b. The idea of contact lenses existed before Fick and Kalt made them.

_____ c. Laser eye surgery is one of the newest treatments for eye problems.

5. **Understanding Main Ideas**

One of the statements below expresses the main idea of the passage. One statement is too general, or too broad. The other explains only part of the passage; it is too narrow. Label the statements M for *main idea*, B for *too broad,* and N for *too narrow.*

_____ a. Many types of contact lenses are available.

_____ b. Many people do not have perfect sight.

_____ c. Eye care has developed over time.

Correct Answers, Part A _____

Correct Answers, Part B _____

Total Correct Answers _____

Herbs: Plants of Many Uses

Since ancient times, people have used plants in many ways. Herbs are plants that have been used most often to flavor food and treat illness. Herbs have also been used as beauty products, fragrances, dyes, and sources of good nutrition. Herbs can come from many different kinds of plants, including trees, shrubs, grasses, and flowering plants. In addition, herbs can come from different plant parts—roots, stems, leaves, or flowers.

Chinese and Egyptian writings from almost 5,000 years ago tell about the use of herbs. Ancient Egyptians used herbs in a number of ways. Herbs were used in food, on the body, and for religious reasons. In China, the emperors Shen Nung and Huang Ti wrote about herbs. They were the first people to write about Chinese herbal medicine. Today, Chinese herbal medicine is used in many parts of the world and for many different kinds of illnesses.

India is another country where herbs have been used for thousands of years. Perfumes and beauty products made with herbs are common in India. Many herbs are used as seasonings in cooking. People in India also have been using herbs as medicine for nearly 5,000 years.

Hundreds of years ago in Europe, people had important reasons for putting herbs in their food. They used herbs to aid digestion and to hide the taste of rotting meat and fish. Herbs were seen as an important part of the diet. Native Americans have been using herbs for hundreds of years. Some of their herbal treatments for disease are still widely used today.

In the 19th century, the ways in which herbs were used as medicines began to change in Europe and the United States. Scientists began to study the chemicals from plants that aided health. Using herbs to treat illnesses can be complex. Each plant gives a different dose of medicine. The season, climate, and soil affect how strong an herb is. Too large a dose of an herbal medicine can result in sickness and sometimes death.

Today, scientists and technical workers make medicines from plants in laboratories. Doctors can give exact doses of these medicines. People can be sure the dosage is safe. Although most medicines are now made in labs, herbs have as many uses as ever. Chamomile shampoo, verbena tea, and aloe vera gels are a few herbal products. People all over the world use herbal products such as these daily.

Reading Time _____

Recalling Facts

1. Herbs have been used as seasonings and medicine
   - ❏ a. from time to time.
   - ❏ b. during the last 2,000 years.
   - ❏ c. since ancient times.

2. Herbs are often used to
   - ❏ a. make food rot.
   - ❏ b. treat illnesses.
   - ❏ c. fertilize gardens.

3. Herbs are obtained
   - ❏ a. from many kinds of plants.
   - ❏ b. mainly from flowers.
   - ❏ c. only from leaves and stems.

4. One recent trend in herbal medicine is
   - ❏ a. scientific study of the chemicals in herbs.
   - ❏ b. the use of chamomile as aspirin.
   - ❏ c. the replacement of manufactured drugs with herbal medicine.

5. Emperors Shen Nung and Huang Ti were the first people to write about
   - ❏ a. medical laboratories.
   - ❏ b. herbs in Indian cooking.
   - ❏ c. Chinese herbal medicine.

Understanding Ideas

6. It is possible to conclude from the article that the use of herbs as medicine is
   - ❏ a. a new idea.
   - ❏ b. an idea with a long history.
   - ❏ c. an idea that was never popular.

7. People use herbs in
   - ❏ a. many parts of the world.
   - ❏ b. few parts of the world.
   - ❏ c. only China and Egypt.

8. Why might technical workers in laboratories be able to create more accurate doses of herbal medicines?
   - ❏ a. They care more about sick people.
   - ❏ b. They are much smarter than other people who work with herbal medicines.
   - ❏ c. They can remove medicine from the herbs and measure its strength.

9. It is possible to conclude from the article that herbs are
   - ❏ a. never harmful.
   - ❏ b. rarely used in cooking.
   - ❏ c. often flavorful.

10. Adding herbs to beauty products is a
    - ❏ a. modern practice with ancient roots.
    - ❏ b. recent trend.
    - ❏ c. practice that no longer exists.

The Art of Herb Gardening

Herb gardens are as beautiful as they are useful. For the herb gardener, the design of a garden is important. Formal gardens may be planted in the shapes of stars, wheels, and interlocking rings. Informal gardens can take on many shapes, often with curving paths.

A gardener plans an herb garden carefully. The amount of time and space available for gardening is crucial. The gardener must also consider the types of herbs to be planted. Will the herbs be used in cooking, as herbal medicines, or for fragrance? The gardener must be especially careful with medicinal herbs, because even small amounts can be poisonous to pets and young children.

To plant an herb garden, the gardener first traces out in the soil the design of the garden. Then the soil is dug, raked, and weeded in the planting area. The gardener plants the herbs according to the needs of each plant. To grow well, different herbs require different amounts of sunlight and space. Newly planted herbs should be watered often. It is important to keep the area free of weeds. The herbs should be trimmed to keep the design of the garden and to keep the plants from flowering. With this care, the herb gardener can be optimistic that the plants will be beautiful, hardy, and useful.

1. **Recognizing Words in Context**

   Find the word *optimistic* in the passage. One definition below is closest to the meaning of that word. One definition has the opposite or nearly opposite meaning. The remaining definition has a completely different meaning. Label the definitions C for *closest*, O for *opposite or nearly opposite*, and D for *different*.

   _____ a. fertile

   _____ b. negative

   _____ c. hopeful

2. **Distinguishing Fact from Opinion**

   Two of the statements below present *facts*, which can be proved correct. The other statement is an *opinion*, which expresses someone's thoughts or beliefs. Label the statements F for *fact* and O for *opinion*.

   _____ a. Designing an herb garden is more difficult than planting it.

   _____ b. Different herbs need different growing conditions.

   _____ c. Trimming an herb before it flowers makes the plant stronger.

3. Keeping Events in Order

Label the statements below 1, 2, and 3 to show the order in which the events happen.

_____ a. The gardener considers what types of herbs to plant.

_____ b. The gardener trims the herbs.

_____ c. The gardener plants the herbs according to the needs of each plant.

4. Making Correct Inferences

Two of the statements below are correct *inferences*, or reasonable guesses. They are based on information in the passage. The other statement is an incorrect, or faulty, inference. Label the statements C for *correct* inference and F for *faulty* inference.

_____ a. Designing and planting an herb garden takes time.

_____ b. Weeds do not help herbs to grow.

_____ c. Only one type of herb should be planted in an herb garden.

5. Understanding Main Ideas

One of the statements below expresses the main idea of the passage. One statement is too general, or too broad. The other explains only part of the passage; it is too narrow. Label the statements M for *main idea*, B for *too broad*, and N for *too narrow*.

_____ a. There are many types of gardens.

_____ b. The design of the garden and the care of the plants are both important to the herb gardener.

_____ c. A gardener should be careful with medicinal herbs.

Correct Answers, Part A _____

Correct Answers, Part B _____

Total Correct Answers _____

Early Discoveries in Electricity

Thousands of years ago in ancient Greece, the scientist Thales made a puzzling discovery. Thales polished a piece of amber and saw that feathers clung to the amber. What Thales saw was an example of static electricity. For another example, think about what happens when a balloon is rubbed on a sweater. When the balloon is held above someone's head, that person's hair stands up.

Static electricity is the result of activity within one of the smallest units of matter. All things are made up of tiny particles called atoms. Within an atom is an even smaller particle called an electron. The electron has a negative charge. This charge causes an electron to pull on things that have a positive charge. Because of electrons, the amber pulls the feathers toward it, and the balloon pulls the hair toward it.

A 3,000-year-old clay vase found in Iraq shows that ancient peoples might have used electricity. The vase contained a copper tube that had an iron rod inside. If the rod and tube were rubbed together, a burst of electricity would be produced.

Most of the electricity used today is in the form of a continuous flow of electrons. Moving electrons form an electric current. Some of the most important early discoveries about electric current were made by Benjamin Franklin. Through his experiments, Franklin revealed several important properties of electric current. In one of these experiments, Franklin showed that electric current exists in nature in the form of lightning.

About 200 years ago, an Italian scientist named Alessandro Volta created the first device that could produce a continuous flow of electric current. Previously, people who needed electricity could only create a brief burst of it by using a hand-cranked generator. They could store a tiny amount of this burst in a container called a Leyden jar.

With Volta's device, no cranking was needed. It was easy to control the power of the current too. Volta stacked small zinc and copper disks in piles. Between each disk, he laid a bit of leather soaked in acid. The chemicals in the acid allowed electrons to flow between the two metals. The flow of electrons produced an electric current. Volta had created the first battery.

Volta's battery led to new discoveries in electricity. The plentiful supply of electricity today is due partly to the work of Franklin, Volta, and other important scientists.

Reading Time _____

Recalling Facts

1. An ancient clay vase holding an iron rod and a copper tube may have been used
   - ❏ a. to prepare food.
   - ❏ b. to create electricity.
   - ❏ c. to make medicine.

2. In ancient times, an important discovery about static electricity was made by
   - ❏ a. Alessandro Volta.
   - ❏ b. Benjamin Franklin.
   - ❏ c. Thales.

3. A small particle with a negative charge is called
   - ❏ a. amber.
   - ❏ b. an electron.
   - ❏ c. zinc.

4. Ben Franklin proved that lightning is
   - ❏ a. a stream of protons.
   - ❏ b. not electricity.
   - ❏ c. an electric current.

5. Alessandro Volta stacked zinc and copper disks to make
   - ❏ a. the first battery.
   - ❏ b. a generator.
   - ❏ c. a lightning experiment.

Understanding Ideas

6. It is possible to conclude from the article that modern uses of electricity depend mostly on
   - ❏ a. static electricity.
   - ❏ b. lightning.
   - ❏ c. electric currents.

7. It is likely that people in the ancient civilization that was part of the region that now includes Iraq
   - ❏ a. knew nothing about electricity.
   - ❏ b. knew something about electricity.
   - ❏ c. knew everything about electricity.

8. Light objects cling to a rubbed balloon or amber stone because of
   - ❏ a. static electricity.
   - ❏ b. zinc atoms.
   - ❏ c. a continuous electric current.

9. The article suggests that the work of early scientists
   - ❏ a. led to modern uses of electricity.
   - ❏ b. seemed important at the time but was later shown to be useless.
   - ❏ c. was not important.

10. A constant flow of electrons produces
   - ❏ a. static electricity.
   - ❏ b. solar power.
   - ❏ c. an electric current.

What Causes Static Electricity?

A balloon that is rubbed on a sweater and held above a person's head will cause hair to stand up on end. So will a wool hat when it is removed. Why? The answer in each case is static electricity. To learn how static electricity works, one must consider atoms and their parts.

All things are made of atoms, including animals, plants, and minerals. Atoms are made up of tiny particles called protons, neutrons, and electrons. While neutrons have no electrical charge, protons and electrons do have charges. Protons have a positive charge, and electrons have a negative charge. An object with a positive charge will attract an object with a negative charge. But two positively charged objects will repel each other, and so will two negatively charged objects.

The charges of protons and electrons balance each other out in most atoms. As a result, the atom itself has no charge. But when a balloon is rubbed on a sweater, electrons move from the atoms of the sweater to the atoms of the balloon. A similar thing happens when a wool hat is pulled off. Electrons from the hair move to the hat. As a result, the atoms of the sweater and the hair that have lost electrons have a positive charge. The balloon and hat, which have gained electrons, have a negative charge. This difference of charges creates static electricity.

1. **Recognizing Words in Context**

   Find the word *repel* in the passage. One definition below is closest to the meaning of that word. One definition has the opposite or nearly opposite meaning. The remaining definition has a completely different meaning. Label the definitions C for *closest*, O for *opposite or nearly opposite*, and D for *different*.

   _____ a. fall down

   _____ b. pull toward

   _____ c. push away

2. **Distinguishing Fact from Opinion**

   Two of the statements below present *facts*, which can be proved correct. The other statement is an *opinion*, which expresses someone's thoughts or beliefs. Label the statements F for *fact* and O for *opinion*.

   _____ a. All things are made up of atoms.

   _____ b. Rubbing a balloon on a sweater is a fun experiment.

   _____ c. Like charges repel, while unlike charges attract.

3. Keeping Events in Order

Label the statements below 1, 2, and 3 to show the order in which the events happen.

_____ a. A balloon is rubbed on a sweater.

_____ b. Electrons move from the atoms of the sweater to the atoms of the balloon.

_____ c. Hair stands on end when the balloon is held near it.

4. Making Correct Inferences

Two of the statements below are correct *inferences*, or reasonable guesses. They are based on information in the passage. The other statement is an incorrect, or faulty, inference. Label the statements C for *correct* inference and F for *faulty* inference.

_____ a. All experiments involving electricity are safe and can be tried by anyone.

_____ b. Static electricity can result when electrons move from the atoms of one object to the atoms of a second object.

_____ c. All things are made up of tiny parts that cannot be seen by the human eye without a powerful microscope.

5. Understanding Main Ideas

One of the statements below expresses the main idea of the passage. One statement is too general, or too broad. The other explains only part of the passage; it is too narrow. Label the statements M for *main idea*, B for *too broad*, and N for *too narrow*.

_____ a. Electrons moving from one object to another create static electricity.

_____ b. Electricity is a part of everyday life.

_____ c. Electrons have a negative charge.

Correct Answers, Part A _____

Correct Answers, Part B _____

Total Correct Answers _____

What Makes a Hurricane?

A hurricane is a powerful storm with strong winds and heavy rains. The word *hurricane* comes from a word of the Taino people of the Caribbean meaning "evil spirit of the wind." People also call hurricanes cyclones or typhoons, especially when they occur in Asia. Meteorologists, scientists who study the weather, use the technical term *tropical cyclones* when talking about hurricanes.

Hurricanes form over the ocean in regions near, but not on, the equator. These storms need just the right conditions to form. The ocean water must be 27°C (80°F) or warmer, and the air must be warm and moist.

Particles of warm air are farther apart than particles of cold air are. Warm air forms a pocket of low pressure, whereas cold air forms a high-pressure area. Hurricanes can form only in areas of low-pressure air. Warm ocean waters heat the low-pressure air, causing it to rise and form tall clouds. As the warmed air rises, high-pressure air rushes in from the sides and creates wind.

The rotation of Earth causes the growing storm to spin. As long as the storm stays over warm water, it continues to grow. If the winds reach a speed of 61 kilometers per hour (38 miles per hour), meteorologists call the storm a tropical storm. If the winds reach a speed of 119 kilometers per hour (74 miles per hour), meteorologists call the storm a hurricane.

A hurricane is shaped like a thick ring with a hollow center. The center is called the eye. Here the winds are calm and the sky is cloudless. Sometimes people make the mistake of thinking a hurricane is over when the eye passes over them. All around the eye are strong winds and tall thunderclouds that produce heavy rains. A hurricane can survive for a few hours or a few weeks. It will not break up or weaken until it moves over cold water or land.

Hurricanes can cause millions of dollars in damage. The powerful winds destroy homes, rip roofs off buildings, break windows, topple trees, and tear down power lines. The storm's heavy rains cause flooding, and so do huge waves created by the strong winds. The sea can rise at least 3 meters (10 feet) during a hurricane in what is called a storm surge. The flooding from a hurricane often kills more people than the winds do.

Reading Time _____

Recalling Facts

1. Meteorologists refer to a hurricane with the technical term
   - ❏ a. tropical cyclone.
   - ❏ b. evil spirit of the wind.
   - ❏ c. tropical storm.

2. A hurricane grows weaker when it moves over
   - ❏ a. warm water.
   - ❏ b. land.
   - ❏ c. tropical oceans.

3. A storm surge occurs when
   - ❏ a. the level of the ocean suddenly rises.
   - ❏ b. heavy rains hit land.
   - ❏ c. strong winds topple trees.

4. A hurricane can form only in an area of
   - ❏ a. cold, dry air.
   - ❏ b. high-pressure air.
   - ❏ c. low-pressure air.

5. A storm with heavy rains and winds of 119 kilometers per hour or more is a
   - ❏ a. thunderstorm.
   - ❏ b. tropical storm.
   - ❏ c. hurricane.

Understanding Ideas

6. If you heard about a storm that had wind speeds of 80 kilometers per hour, you could infer that it was a
   - ❏ a. hurricane.
   - ❏ b. tropical storm.
   - ❏ c. storm surge.

7. It is possible to conclude from the article that a hurricane could form
   - ❏ a. over a large desert.
   - ❏ b. above an icy lake.
   - ❏ c. over the Atlantic Ocean.

8. The article suggests that most people who are killed during hurricanes die as a result of
   - ❏ a. drowning.
   - ❏ b. being struck by flying objects.
   - ❏ c. burns.

9. It is possible to conclude from the article that hurricanes are storms that
   - ❏ a. can kill.
   - ❏ b. are harmless.
   - ❏ c. are occasionally dangerous.

10. The article suggests that hurricanes form
    - ❏ a. everywhere in the world.
    - ❏ b. over every body of water in the world.
    - ❏ c. only in certain regions.

The Day of the Hurricane

Mrs. Timms listened as the radio announcer issued a hurricane warning for her town. Then she woke up her sons, Eddie and Jasper, and quickly explained, "We've got a lot to do, boys. There is no school today, and my office is closed. The hurricane is coming!"

Just then, the boys' grandfather arrived from his seaside home. Grandpa explained that the sheriff's deputies had told people to evacuate their homes. It just wasn't safe for anyone to stay near the ocean during the hurricane.

Soon afterward, Mrs. Timms left to buy supplies the family would need during the storm. Batteries, bottled water, and canned food were a few of the items on her list.

Grandpa stayed with the boys, and the three of them made preparations for the storm. First they filled the bathtub and all the empty water bottles they could find. Next, they unplugged almost everything in the house. Then Eddie helped Grandpa board up the windows. Meanwhile, Jasper put the outdoor chairs and his bicycle in the shed.

Later, as the storm approached, the family stayed in protected areas away from the windows and outside walls. Mrs. Timms and Grandpa moved chairs to a protected space near the staircase. Eddie and Jasper sat under a sturdy table next to them, reading and playing games. They waited for the radio announcer to declare that the hurricane had passed.

1. Recognizing Words in Context

Find the word *evacuate* in the passage. One definition below is closest to the meaning of that word. One definition has the opposite or nearly opposite meaning. The remaining definition has a completely different meaning. Label the definitions C for *closest*, O for *opposite or nearly opposite*, and D for *different*.

_____ a. arrive

_____ b. leave

_____ c. lock

2. Distinguishing Fact from Opinion

Two of the statements below present *facts*, which can be proved correct. The other statement is an *opinion*, which expresses someone's thoughts or beliefs. Label the statements F for *fact* and O for *opinion*.

_____ a. Hurricanes are the scariest storms.

_____ b. One way to stay safe during a hurricane is to stay away from windows.

_____ c. Hurricanes often cause damage to homes.

3. Keeping Events in Order

Label the statements below 1, 2, and 3 to show the order in which the events happen.

_____ a. Eddie helps Grandpa board up the windows.

_____ b. The family waits for the radio announcer to declare that the storm is over.

_____ c. Mrs. Timms leaves to buy supplies.

4. Making Correct Inferences

Two of the statements below are correct *inferences,* or reasonable guesses. They are based on information in the passage. The other statement is an incorrect, or faulty, inference. Label the statements C for *correct* inference and F for *faulty* inference.

_____ a. Grandpa filled the bathtub because he was worried that the storm might disrupt the water supply.

_____ b. Grandpa put boards on the windows because the glass was broken.

_____ c. Grandpa unplugged the appliances in case there was lightning during the storm.

5. Understanding Main Ideas

One of the statements below expresses the main idea of the passage. One statement is too general, or too broad. The other explains only part of the passage; it is too narrow. Label the statements M for *main idea,* B for *too broad,* and N for *too narrow.*

_____ a. Fresh batteries are helpful if the power goes out during a hurricane.

_____ b. There is a lot to do to prepare for a hurricane.

_____ c. It's wise to be prepared for dangerous events.

Correct Answers, Part A _____

Correct Answers, Part B _____

Total Correct Answers _____

Where Have All the Grasslands Gone?

Grasslands in the United States once stretched from the Mississippi River to the Rocky Mountains. The grasslands, also called prairies, were home to grasses, herbs, birds, rodents, and grazers. By eating grass, grazers such as buffalo, deer, and elk kept it from taking over. Fires helped to maintain grasslands too. Fires cleared out old or dead grass so that new grass could grow. Plants and animals of the grasslands relied on one another for life. For thousands of years, Native Americans were a part of this ecosystem. All of the things they needed to live could be found on the grasslands.

Today, there are just small islands of grassland left. Most of the grasslands have been plowed under, paved over, or used for cattle. What led to the destruction of grasslands that once covered almost half of the country?

First, pioneers moving west found the fertile soil of the grasslands to be perfect for farming. A new type of plow allowed pioneer farmers to cut through the dense roots of the grass with ease.

A second cause for the change in the grasslands had to do with the buffalo. Pioneers began to hunt buffalo for sport. Over 100 years, the number of buffalo fell from about 60,000,000 to 1,000. Without the grazing of the buffalo, there was nothing to keep certain kinds of plants from growing out of control and crowding out other plants.

The crops planted in the region are a third cause for the change in the land. Without the dense roots of grasses growing in it, the soil had nothing holding it down during winter. In the 1920s there was much less rain than normal, and the dry soil began to blow away. To control this soil erosion, the U.S. government began to buy back land from farmers. In 1960, about 4 million acres (1.6 million hectares) of this land were deemed national grasslands.

Today people are working to restore grasslands, and they are carefully trying to re-create the original conditions. They plant combinations of grasses and other plants that once grew on the prairies. They set controlled fires to learn more about how fires keep the sites healthy. They bring in buffalo to live and graze on the sites. With more study, they hope to learn as much as they can. The goal is to best protect and manage the small regions of grassland we have left.

Reading Time _____

Recalling Facts

1. Grasslands once covered
   - ❑ a. the world.
   - ❑ b. almost half of the United States.
   - ❑ c. the entire United States.

2. For thousands of years, _____ living on the grasslands had everything they needed to live.
   - ❑ a. pioneer farmers
   - ❑ b. Native Americans
   - ❑ c. cattle ranchers

3. In the 1920s, soil erosion occurred in places where
   - ❑ a. grasslands had been replaced by farms.
   - ❑ b. tall grasses crowded out other plants.
   - ❑ c. buffalo had eaten all the grass.

4. Pioneers moving west
   - ❑ a. found the grasslands to be perfect farmland.
   - ❑ b. found that the grasslands were not worth farming.
   - ❑ c. protected buffalo from hunters.

5. Grasslands are made up of
   - ❑ a. large trees and mountains.
   - ❑ b. swamps and marshes.
   - ❑ c. grasses and herbs.

Understanding Ideas

6. According to the information in the article, if you were walking through a prairie, which animal would you be most likely to see?
   - ❑ a. a lion
   - ❑ b. a goat
   - ❑ c. a rabbit

7. The article suggests that people can help restore grasslands by
   - ❑ a. keeping buffalo off protected sites.
   - ❑ b. bringing buffalo to live on protected sites.
   - ❑ c. hunting buffalo.

8. It is possible to conclude from the article that not all of the grasslands will be restored because
   - ❑ a. most of the soil has been poisoned with weed killers.
   - ❑ b. some people want to use the land for other things.
   - ❑ c. buffalo have become extinct.

9. A natural part of a healthy grassland is
   - ❑ a. fire.
   - ❑ b. plowing.
   - ❑ c. ranching.

10. The article suggests that some grasslands will
    - ❑ a. disappear forever.
    - ❑ b. never be in danger.
    - ❑ c. be restored and protected.

Hunting Buffalo: A Way of Life

Native Americans of the Great Plains hunted buffalo, sometimes called bison, to survive. The buffalo provided almost everything they needed to live. At first, Plains hunters used arrows and spears to kill buffalo. These men herded buffalo into traps where they were easy to kill. Later, the men hunted buffalo on horseback with guns.

After a hunt, it was the women in most tribes who butchered the buffalo. The animal, which had an average weight of about 900 kilograms (2,000 pounds), was conveyed to camp in pieces. The women cut out the meat and organs for food. They removed heavy skins in one or two pieces.

Fresh meat and organs were made into dishes such as calf and vegetable stew or roasted udder filled with buffalo milk. Some meat was dried to make buffalo jerky or pounded and mixed with fat to make pemmican. Jerky and pemmican were eaten when fresh meat was gone.

Plains women tanned skins from the hunt. The process took up to 10 days. The tanned hides were used to make tipi covers, clothing, blankets, bags, and diapers.

Native peoples used all parts of the buffalo. Knives, arrowheads, and needles were made from bone. Cups and spoons were carved from horn. Glue and rattles were made from hooves. Native Americans of the Plains even found a use for the buffalo tail—as a flyswatter!

1. Recognizing Words in Context

Find the word *conveyed* in the passage. One definition below is closest to the meaning of that word. One definition has the opposite or nearly opposite meaning. The remaining definition has a completely different meaning. Label the definitions C for *closest*, O for *opposite or nearly opposite*, and D for *different*.

_____ a. carried

_____ b. cut up

_____ c. abandoned

2. Distinguishing Fact from Opinion

Two of the statements below present *facts*, which can be proved correct. The other statement is an *opinion*, which expresses someone's thoughts or beliefs. Label the statements F for *fact* and O for *opinion*.

_____ a. Buffalo jerky is made from dried meat.

_____ b. Native Americans of the Plains hunted buffalo.

_____ c. The use of so many buffalo parts was very clever.

3. Keeping Events in Order

Label the statements below 1, 2, and 3 to show the order in which the events happened.

_____ a. Hunters herded buffalo into traps to kill them.

_____ b. Buffalo parts were carried back to camp.

_____ c. The buffalo were cut into pieces.

4. Making Correct Inferences

Two of the statements below are correct *inferences,* or reasonable guesses. They are based on information in the passage. The other statement is an incorrect, or faulty, inference. Label the statements C for *correct* inference and F for *faulty* inference.

_____ a. Native Americans of the Plains were wasteful with buffalo.

_____ b. Lots of different dishes could be made from buffalo meat.

_____ c. Native Americans of the Plains could get most of the things they needed from buffalo.

5. Understanding Main Ideas

One of the statements below expresses the main idea of the passage. One statement is too general, or too broad. The other explains only part of the passage; it is too narrow. Label the statements M for *main idea,* B for *too broad,* and N for *too narrow.*

_____ a. Native Americans of the Plains had a number of ways to hunt buffalo.

_____ b. Hunting buffalo gave Native Americans of the Plains the things they needed to live.

_____ c. Native Americans depended on their natural surroundings to survive.

Correct Answers, Part A _____

Correct Answers, Part B _____

Total Correct Answers _____

An arachnid has legs with joints, a tough outer skeleton, and no backbone. Insects share these traits with arachnids. They are related. However, animals grouped as arachnids have several other things in common with one another. All arachnids have eight walking legs, simple eyes, and a body made up of one or two sections. They eat food in fluid form. They often live alone on land and kill the food they eat. Arachnids include spiders, scorpions, ticks, mites, and daddy longlegs.

Like most other arachnids, spiders have eight walking legs, fangs, and palps for feeling. The two sections of the body of a spider are the head and the abdomen. All spiders spin a silklike substance made from protein, but not all spiders make webs. Some spiders, such as wolf spiders, hunt insects. Other spiders wait for insects to land in their webs. Spiders kill insects in two ways. Some spiders wrap the insects in silk and tear them apart, whereas others kill insects with venom from their hollow fangs. The venom dissolves the insides of the insect, and the spider sucks the liquid out.

A scorpion is recognizable by its lobsterlike front pincers and curved tail. The tail is tipped with a poisonous stinger that can be very painful to humans. The stinger is used mostly for defense. Scorpions come out at night and wait for prey to approach. They eat anything they can catch, mostly insects and other arachnids. Scorpions sometimes use their stingers to kill larger prey. Smaller prey is just held and eaten without being stung. Scorpions tear apart their prey, cover the parts with digestive juices, wait for the parts to turn to liquid, and suck the liquid into their stomachs.

Ticks and mites have only a single body section. Most ticks and mites have six legs when they hatch from eggs. They grow another pair of legs as they develop into adults. Ticks and mites often feed on other living things. They have mouth parts for sucking blood and juices. Ticks feed on the blood of reptiles, birds, and mammals. Mites feed on blood, skin, and other animal and plant materials.

Daddy longlegs, also called harvestmen, have some unique features. They can take in small particles of food in addition to liquid foods. To catch insect prey, daddy longlegs run after it. Another fact that sets daddy longlegs apart from most arachnids is that they also feed on plants.

Reading Time _____

Recalling Facts

1. An animal with eight walking legs that eats food in fluid form is
   - ❏ a. an arachnid.
   - ❏ b. a squid.
   - ❏ c. an insect.

2. Arachnids have
   - ❏ a. compound eyes.
   - ❏ b. simple eyes.
   - ❏ c. no eyes.

3. All spiders
   - ❏ a. make webs.
   - ❏ b. spin a silklike substance.
   - ❏ c. eat plants.

4. Plant material is eaten by
   - ❏ a. spiders and scorpions.
   - ❏ b. all arachnids.
   - ❏ c. daddy longlegs.

5. A scorpion
   - ❏ a. builds a web to catch prey.
   - ❏ b. always uses its stinger to kill prey.
   - ❏ c. waits for its prey to approach.

Understanding Ideas

6. It is possible to conclude from the article that all insects and spiders have
   - ❏ a. tough outer skeletons.
   - ❏ b. three body segments.
   - ❏ c. four legs.

7. The use of venom to kill prey is most common in
   - ❏ a. animals with fur.
   - ❏ b. all arachnids.
   - ❏ c. spiders and scorpions.

8. From the context you can infer that the word *trait* means
   - ❏ a. body part.
   - ❏ b. characteristic.
   - ❏ c. type of insect.

9. It is possible to conclude from the article that almost all adult arachnids
   - ❏ a. kill their prey with venom.
   - ❏ b. have four pairs of legs.
   - ❏ c. are dangerous to humans.

10. Grouping animals together based on shared traits helps people understand
    - ❏ a. how animals are similar and different.
    - ❏ b. how animals find food.
    - ❏ c. how humans are different from other animals.

Not all spiders wait for prey to fall into their webs. The bolas spider swings a sticky silken thread to catch moths. First it attaches a line of silk to a leaf or twig. The spider uses its hind legs to pull the silk from the tip of its abdomen. Next, the spider lets out a second silk thread up to 60 centimeters (24 inches) long. This thread is coated with sticky droplets. The bolas spider hangs upside down from the first line of silk and dangles the sticky line from a single leg. Then, to lure its prey, the spider emits an odor similar to one given off by a female moth. When a male moth comes toward the smell, the bolas spider swings or throws the sticky line to trap the moth.

The ogre-faced spider throws a small web to catch its prey. At night, this spider makes a silken net. First it spins a flat web about the size of a quarter to use as the net. Then the spider takes the web in its front legs and watches for prey. When an insect approaches, the spider throws the net to trap it. The spider enjoys its meal and finds a twig to rest on until its next night of hunting.

1. **Recognizing Words in Context**

Find the word *emits* in the passage. One definition below is closest to the meaning of that word. One definition has the opposite or nearly opposite meaning. The remaining definition has a completely different meaning. Label the definitions C for *closest,* O for *opposite or nearly opposite,* and D for *different.*

_____ a. deletes

_____ b. releases

_____ c. absorbs

2. **Distinguishing Fact from Opinion**

Two of the statements below present *facts,* which can be proved correct. The other statement is an *opinion,* which expresses someone's thoughts or beliefs. Label the statements F for *fact* and O for *opinion.*

_____ a. A bolas spider uses a scent to attract prey.

_____ b. The design of the ogre-faced spider's web is clever.

_____ c. Spiders use their webs in different ways.

3. **Keeping Events in Order**

Label the statements below 1, 2, and 3 to show the order in which the events happen.

_____ a. The bolas spider dangles a sticky thread from one leg.

_____ b. The bolas spider attaches a silk thread to a leaf.

_____ c. The bolas spider gives off an odor to attract male moths.

4. **Making Correct Inferences**

Two of the statements below are correct *inferences,* or reasonable guesses. They are based on information in the passage. The other statement is an incorrect, or faulty, inference. Label the statements C for *correct* inference and F for *faulty* inference.

_____ a. All spiders use complex webs to catch prey.

_____ b. Spiders have a number of ways of catching insects.

_____ c. A spider can catch prey with a single silk line.

5. **Understanding Main Ideas**

One of the statements below expresses the main idea of the passage. One statement is too general, or too broad. The other explains only part of the passage; it is too narrow. Label the statements M for *main idea,* B for *too broad,* and N for *too narrow.*

_____ a. The ogre-faced spider makes a net that is about the size of a quarter.

_____ b. Spiders hunt in a number of ways.

_____ c. Some spiders throw webs to catch their prey.

Correct Answers, Part A _____

Correct Answers, Part B _____

Total Correct Answers _____

Training to Be an Astronaut

Astronauts come from a variety of professions. Teachers, authors, doctors, scientists, and pilots are some of the people who have become astronauts. They share a love of science, a sense of adventure, and extensive training. To get into the U.S. space program, a person must have a strong background in math or science. A person also has to pass medical tests, fitness tests, and mental tests. The space program looks for people in good health who work well with others.

The National Aeronautics and Space Administration, or NASA, runs the space program. Even when NASA invites a person to join the space program, that person is not yet an astronaut. First, new recruits go through a year of classroom training. They learn how a space shuttle works. They study weather, space, and computers. If they do well, they are accepted as astronauts.

A new astronaut goes through years of special training. New astronauts might work with scientists making shuttle equipment or work with mission control to contact crews in space. These tasks give them skills that come in handy during space missions.

Some astronauts know how to fly jets when they enter the program. They maintain their skills by flying often. Astronauts who do not know how to fly receive pilot training. All astronauts need to learn how to fly a space shuttle using the shuttle control panels. They also practice landing an aircraft similar to the shuttle.

Underwater training exercises help astronauts to feel what it is like to move around in a space suit. To experience weightlessness, astronauts ride in a jet nicknamed "the vomit comet." The jet repeatedly climbs high into the air and then plunges into dives of up to 3 kilometers (2 miles). During these long dives, astronauts experience weightlessness for 30 to 60 seconds. The jet might dive 40 times in a day. Some astronauts feel sick to their stomachs after a while.

Astronauts have to be prepared for any kind of emergency on a mission. They learn all kinds of survival skills. These skills include parachuting over land and water, rafting, and camping with only a small survival kit.

After years of training, astronauts are assigned to a mission. They then train with other members of the crew to prepare for a mission. Most of the missions require the astronauts to perform important experiments in space.

Reading Time _____

Recalling Facts

1. To enter the space program, a person must
   - ❑ a. pass a medical and fitness test.
   - ❑ b. already have experience as an astronaut.
   - ❑ c. be a teacher.

2. New recruits spend their first year in the space program in
   - ❑ a. space.
   - ❑ b. a weightless room.
   - ❑ c. the classroom.

3. Learning to fly and land a shuttle is a skill
   - ❑ a. only shuttle pilots learn.
   - ❑ b. none of the astronauts learn.
   - ❑ c. all of the astronauts learn.

4. Astronauts are assigned to a shuttle mission
   - ❑ a. after years of training in the space program.
   - ❑ b. as soon as they enter the space program.
   - ❑ c. after two months of training in the space program.

5. Astronauts train in an underwater tank to practice
   - ❑ a. holding their breath.
   - ❑ b. space walking and moving in a space suit.
   - ❑ c. building endurance for liftoffs.

Understanding Ideas

6. One skill an astronaut learns in training is how to
   - ❑ a. speak foreign languages.
   - ❑ b. ride a bicycle.
   - ❑ c. fly a shuttle using the shuttle control panels.

7. Astronauts fly on special jets to
   - ❑ a. experience weightlessness.
   - ❑ b. relax and have fun.
   - ❑ c. train for their physical exams.

8. The article suggests that people in poor health
   - ❑ a. are surprisingly good astronauts.
   - ❑ b. often become astronauts.
   - ❑ c. will not be chosen to become astronauts.

9. It is possible to conclude from the article that a new astronaut in the space program
   - ❑ a. flies on a shuttle mission right away to gain experience.
   - ❑ b. works in the space program to gain knowledge.
   - ❑ c. knows a lot and does not need to learn new things.

10. It is possible to conclude from the article that astronauts have
    - ❑ a. no training.
    - ❑ b. little training.
    - ❑ c. a great deal of training.

Disappointments and Triumphs of Female Astronauts

In the early 1960s, thirteen women passed the tests used to admit new astronauts into the space program. The top female candidate, Geraldyn Cobb, received a score of "excellent" on the flight test and broke a test record on one of the mental tests. Cobb and other women proved their skills through the tests. They showed they had the talent to become excellent astronauts. In spite of this, the men in charge of NASA decided not to allow the women to join the space program. The astronauts they chose were all men.

It was not until 1978 that NASA allowed women to join the space program. The new female astronauts had exemplary skills, just as Geraldyn Cobb had had. These skills were greatly needed. The number of astronauts being sent into space was growing.

In 1983, Sally Ride became the first U.S. woman in space. On her first mission, Ride watched for problems on the shuttle. She also sent two satellites into space.

Women have contributed much to the space program. Women achieved some great firsts in the 1990s. For example, Eileen Collins was the first woman to pilot the space shuttle. Women today continue to bring superb skills and great accomplishments to the space program.

1. **Recognizing Words in Context**

   Find the word *exemplary* in the passage. One definition below is closest to the meaning of that word. One definition has the opposite or nearly opposite meaning. The remaining definition has a completely different meaning. Label the definitions C for *closest*, O for *opposite or nearly opposite*, and D for *different*.

   _____ a. technical

   _____ b. weak

   _____ c. excellent

2. **Distinguishing Fact from Opinion**

   Two of the statements below present *facts*, which can be proved correct. The other statement is an *opinion*, which expresses someone's thoughts or beliefs. Label the statements F for *fact* and O for *opinion*.

   _____ a. Women make fine astronauts.

   _____ b. In 1978, women joined the space program for the first time.

   _____ c. The first female shuttle pilot was Eileen Collins.

3. **Keeping Events in Order**

   Label the statements below 1, 2, and 3 to show the order in which the events happened.

   _____ a. Thirteen women passed astronaut entrance tests in the early 1960s.

   _____ b. Geraldyn Cobb was not allowed to join the space program.

   _____ c. Sally Ride became the first U.S. woman in space.

4. **Making Correct Inferences**

   Two of the statements below are correct *inferences*, or reasonable guesses. They are based on information in the passage. The other statement is an incorrect, or faulty, inference. Label the statements C for *correct* inference and F for *faulty* inference.

   _____ a. Female astronauts perform many tasks in the space program.

   _____ b. Geraldyn Cobb did not have the skills to be an astronaut.

   _____ c. The space program did not let women become astronauts before 1978.

5. **Understanding Main Ideas**

   One of the statements below expresses the main idea of the passage. One statement is too general, or too broad. The other explains only part of the passage; it is too narrow. Label the statements M for *main idea*, B for *too broad*, and N for *too narrow*.

   _____ a. Women have the skills needed for many different types of work.

   _____ b. In spite of their skills, women in the early 1960s were not asked to be astronauts.

   _____ c. Even though women were at first turned away, they have succeeded as astronauts.

Correct Answers, Part A _____

Correct Answers, Part B _____

Total Correct Answers _____

What Good Is Sleep?

The human body needs sleep to stay in good health. Not sleeping well can cause a person to feel more than just tired. Lack of sleep can also make it difficult to think clearly. The person may feel as if he or she has no energy. Some people may become moody and bad tempered without deep sleep. To find out why the human body needs to sleep, scientists study body activities and brain waves during sleep.

Scientists suspect that there are several reasons that people need to sleep. One theory is that sleep restores energy and gives the body and mind time to recover from the day's activities. Some scientists believe that the main purpose of sleep is to allow the body to save energy.

Different types of sleep may have different effects on the body and mind. There are two types of sleep—quiet sleep and active sleep.

As people fall asleep, they move through the four stages of quiet sleep. In the first stage, the muscles relax, but the mind is still aware of its surroundings. In stage two, the heart rate and breathing slow down. The mind is no longer aware of the outside world. In stages three and four, the mind and body continue to slow down, and muscles relax completely. Stage four is the deepest period of quiet sleep.

During quiet sleep, the body moves from stages one to four and then backward to stages two or one again. It moves back to stage four, and then, after about an hour and a half of quiet sleep, the body moves into active sleep.

During active sleep, mind and body functions speed up. This type of sleep is sometimes called dreaming sleep. Most dreaming occurs during active sleep. Scientists call active sleep REM, or rapid eye movement, sleep. During this stage, the eyes move back and forth very quickly under the eyelids. The body stays in active sleep for less than half an hour. Then it begins the stages of quiet sleep again.

Throughout a night of sleep, the cycle of quiet sleep and active sleep repeats many times. Each type of sleep is needed for a person to feel well rested, but scientists believe the two types help the body in different ways. They believe that quiet sleep restores energy to the body and that active sleep restores the mental energy needed for learning and clear thinking.

Reading Time _____

Recalling Facts

1. The two types of sleep are known as
   - ❑ a. deep sleep and tired sleep.
   - ❑ b. quiet sleep and active sleep.
   - ❑ c. dreaming sleep and waking sleep.

2. As people fall asleep, they move through the four stages of
   - ❑ a. dreaming sleep.
   - ❑ b. active sleep.
   - ❑ c. quiet sleep.

3. Scientists also call active sleep
   - ❑ a. rapid eye movement sleep.
   - ❑ b. sleepwalking.
   - ❑ c. restless sleep.

4. Most dreaming occurs
   - ❑ a. before falling asleep.
   - ❑ b. during quiet sleep.
   - ❑ c. during active sleep.

5. The cycle of quiet sleep and active sleep happens
   - ❑ a. three times a night.
   - ❑ b. once a night.
   - ❑ c. many times a night.

Understanding Ideas

6. The article suggests that not sleeping well can cause a person to feel
   - ❑ a. energized.
   - ❑ b. hungry.
   - ❑ c. low on energy.

7. It is possible to conclude from the article that studying how the body sleeps helps scientists understand
   - ❑ a. why people need sleep.
   - ❑ b. how people can do without sleep.
   - ❑ c. why sleep is often harmful.

8. The article suggests that quiet sleep and active sleep
   - ❑ a. restore energy in different ways.
   - ❑ b. restore energy in the same way.
   - ❑ c. do not restore energy.

9. It is likely that a person who had quiet sleep without active sleep for a few nights would
   - ❑ a. have very tired muscles.
   - ❑ b. not have the usual amount of mental energy.
   - ❑ c. be more rested than usual.

10. It is possible to conclude from the article that sleep is
    - ❑ a. needed to function well.
    - ❑ b. not needed to function well.
    - ❑ c. more important as one gets older.

Helpful Hints for Falling Asleep

When people are having trouble falling asleep, they often focus too hard on falling asleep. Some people become worried or scared because they cannot sleep. The truth is that a night or two without sleep can be frustrating, but it is not harmful. Remembering this can help one to unwind and let the mind rest.

Sleep experts suggest that people who are having trouble falling asleep let their thoughts wander while they are in bed. If the mind is racing, a person can use mind games to calm these thoughts. Counting works well for some people. Others imagine they are floating like a leaf down toward the ground. Sometimes a bad thought or a worry won't leave the mind. Turning on the light and writing about the problem may help a person to let it go. In the same way, reading or listening to soft music can help a person let go of stress and worries.

If none of these in-bed techniques help, a person may need to get up and unwind in another way. Stretching or taking a hot bath can help one to relax. Other experts suggest reading in another room until it becomes difficult to keep the eyes open.

It is also important not to eat or drink anything containing caffeine within an hour or two of going to bed. Chocolate or caffeinated soft drinks can make it hard to sleep.

1. Recognizing Words in Context

Find the word *unwind* in the passage. One definition below is closest to the meaning of that word. One definition has the opposite or nearly opposite meaning. The remaining definition has a completely different meaning. Label the definitions C for *closest*, O for *opposite or nearly opposite,* and D for *different.*

_____ a. relax

_____ b. become tense

_____ c. repeat

2. Distinguishing Fact from Opinion

Two of the statements below present *facts,* which can be proved correct. The other statement is an *opinion,* which expresses someone's thoughts or beliefs. Label the statements F for *fact* and O for *opinion.*

_____ a. Sleep experts suggest reading as a way to fall asleep.

_____ b. Caffeine makes it more difficult for the body to fall asleep.

_____ c. A night without sleep is an awful experience.

3. Keeping Events in Order

Label the statements below 1, 2, and 3 to show the order in which the events happen.

_____ a. A person drifts off to sleep.

_____ b. A person lies down and tries to fall asleep by allowing thoughts to wander.

_____ c. Unable to fall asleep, a person takes a hot bath to relax.

4. Making Correct Inferences

Two of the statements below are correct *inferences,* or reasonable guesses. They are based on information in the passage. The other statement is an incorrect, or faulty, inference. Label the statements C for *correct* inference and F for *faulty* inference.

_____ a. The key to falling asleep is to unwind and let the mind relax.

_____ b. A person may have to try several different ways of falling asleep.

_____ c. It is always necessary to get out of bed in order to unwind and fall asleep.

5. Understanding Main Ideas

One of the statements below expresses the main idea of the passage. One statement is too general, or too broad. The other explains only part of the passage; it is too narrow. Label the statements M for *main idea,* B for *too broad,* and N for *too narrow.*

_____ a. The right amount of sleep is necessary for good health.

_____ b. Writing can help a person let go of a problem.

_____ c. There are a number of techniques that help people fall asleep.

Correct Answers, Part A _____

Correct Answers, Part B _____

Total Correct Answers _____

       How Sedimentary Rock Forms

Sedimentary rock is a type of rock that covers about three-fourths of Earth's land surface. It is formed when minerals and other matter are deposited in layers. These layers, called strata, can be seen clearly in steep rock walls such as those found in the Grand Canyon.

There are many different kinds of sedimentary rock. Each kind forms in a different way. Some sedimentary rocks form as wind and water leave behind small bits of rock and sand. Others form from chemicals or from the remains of living things.

The most common kinds of sedimentary rock consist of deposits left behind by water. The water wears away rocks and carries away sand and small bits of rock. These minerals are deposited in many places. Over time, the deposits build up into layers. Over thousands of years, old layers of matter are covered by new layers. The weight of the layers presses the bits of rock together. Water seeps through the layers, leaving minerals that cement the bits together to form rock.

Some of the rocks formed by water, wind, and glaciers are sandstone, loess, and tillite. Sandstone is formed by grains of sand left behind by water. Huge sandstone formations can be seen in Monument Valley in Arizona. Crumbly rock formed from the dust blown by the wind is called loess. This yellow rock covers large regions of the world. A rock made up of large bits of rock that have combined together is called tillite. The shifting ice fields of glaciers form tillite.

Most kinds of sedimentary rock are formed by water alone. Minerals in the water build up over time. As the water flows, these minerals are left behind. Stalactites and stalagmites found in caves are made up of rock formed in this way. Travertine is another rock of this type. It is formed by water flowing from hot springs. Travertine formations at Mammoth Hot Springs in Yellowstone National Park look like the terraces of a palace.

Sedimentary rock can even form from the remains of living things. Chalk and coal are two kinds of rock that form in this way. Chalk forms from animal skeletons and shells that gather on the floor of the sea. Coal is formed from the remains of plants. Over time, the layers of dead matter become solid chalk and coal. All sedimentary rock takes thousands—or even millions—of years to form.

Reading Time _____

Recalling Facts

1. The most common kinds of sedimentary rock form from deposits left behind by
   ❑ a. water.
   ❑ b. wind.
   ❑ c. plants.

2. Stalactites and stalagmites are made up of rock formed by
   ❑ a. the sun.
   ❑ b. the wind.
   ❑ c. water.

3. Chalk and coal are sedimentary rocks made up of
   ❑ a. the remains of living things.
   ❑ b. sand.
   ❑ c. gemstones.

4. Sedimentary rock forms
   ❑ a. overnight.
   ❑ b. over 10 to 20 years.
   ❑ c. over thousands of years.

5. Sedimentary rock covers
   ❑ a. a small part of Earth's surface.
   ❑ b. a third of Earth's surface.
   ❑ c. about three-fourths of Earth's land surface.

Understanding Ideas

6. It is possible to conclude from the article that sedimentary rock forms from matter deposited
   ❑ a. into deep holes.
   ❑ b. in tall piles.
   ❑ c. in layers.

7. The article suggests that sedimentary rocks such as sandstone, travertine, and coal form
   ❑ a. in the same way.
   ❑ b. in different ways.
   ❑ c. from the same materials.

8. Most sedimentary rocks consist of
   ❑ a. minerals that were once part of other rocks.
   ❑ b. minerals that come directly from lava.
   ❑ c. minerals found in caves.

9. The article suggests that sedimentary rock formations can
   ❑ a. be seen in many different kinds of places.
   ❑ b. be seen mainly underwater.
   ❑ c. no longer be seen in most part of the worlds.

10. It is possible to conclude from the article that all types of sedimentary rock form from
    ❑ a. exactly the same materials.
    ❑ b. layers of matter left behind over time.
    ❑ c. the force of the wind.

Fossils: A Record of Life on Earth

A fossil is the remains of a living thing preserved in stone. Fossils take thousands or even millions of years to form. Most plants and animals die without leaving a trace, but some form fossils. Most fossils are found in sedimentary rock. As the water from a river or other body of water moves, it leaves behind layers of sand and silt. From time to time, plant or animal remains are buried in the sand. As the layers press down on one another, the sand turns into rock. In this process, some of the remains become fossils. The buried remains leave a stone imprint or a solid stone copy in the rock.

As a result of the formation of fossils, sedimentary rock contains a record of life on Earth. Older fossils are found in lower layers of rock. Newer fossils are found in layers near the top. Scientists study fossils from different layers to learn how life has changed over time. They have found that life forms have become more intricate. In one case, scientists studied fossils in the rock walls of the Grand Canyon. Fossils found in bottom layers from a billion years ago show only algae. Fossils found in top layers from 300 million years ago show animal tracks. With the help of fossils, it is easier to understand how living things evolved on Earth.

1. **Recognizing Words in Context**

Find the word *intricate* in the passage. One definition below is closest to the meaning of that word. One definition has the opposite or nearly opposite meaning. The remaining definition has a completely different meaning. Label the definitions C for *closest*, O for *opposite or nearly opposite*, and D for *different*.

_____ a. strong

_____ b. simple

_____ c. complex

2. **Distinguishing Fact from Opinion**

Two of the statements below present *facts*, which can be proved correct. The other statement is an *opinion*, which expresses someone's thoughts or beliefs. Label the statements F for *fact* and O for *opinion*.

_____ a. Fossils are found in sedimentary rock.

_____ b. Looking for fossils is a lot of fun.

_____ c. Fossils provide a record of life on Earth.

3. Keeping Events in Order

Label the statements below 1, 2, and 3 to show the order in which the events happen.

_____ a. Scientists find fossils in sedimentary rock.

_____ b. Animal remains are buried in layers of sand.

_____ c. Scientists study fossils to learn about the history of life on Earth.

4. Making Correct Inferences

Two of the statements below are correct *inferences,* or reasonable guesses. They are based on information in the passage. The other statement is an incorrect, or faulty, inference. Label the statements C for *correct* inference and F for *faulty* inference.

_____ a. Every living thing leaves a fossil when it dies.

_____ b. Fossils reveal a great deal about the history of Earth.

_____ c. Without fossils, scientists would know much less about the history of life on Earth.

5. Understanding Main Ideas

One of the statements below expresses the main idea of the passage. One statement is too general, or too broad. The other explains only part of the passage; it is too narrow. Label the statements M for *main idea,* B for *too broad,* and N for *too narrow.*

_____ a. Most fossils are found in sedimentary rock.

_____ b. Beneath the surface of Earth lies much information about life in the past.

_____ c. Fossils are an important source of information for scientists.

Correct Answers, Part A _____

Correct Answers, Part B _____

Total Correct Answers _____

11   A   Surviving the Tides

For the animals and plants living at the seashore, each day is a struggle. The seashore is a land of extremes, with features that may include large rocks and sand dunes, along with the open ocean. The ebb and flow of the tides make the seashore a place of constant change. Sea life covered by water in the morning may be left in dry sand under the heat of the sun by afternoon. How does life survive in this harsh environment?

About every 12 hours, the tide reaches its farthest point up the shore. This is high tide, and most of the beach is under water. Some forms of sea life cling tightly to rocks so that the crashing waves do not carry them to shore. A sea snail uses its foot like a suction cup to grip rocks. Tough-shelled barnacles produce a substance that cements their shells to rock. Instead of having roots like a plant, seaweed has a part called a holdfast that attaches to rocks or the sea bottom.

Nevertheless, as the water level goes down with the receding tide, some sea life is left behind on the shore. Sea urchins, sea stars, and seaweed are a few of the living things that may die if trapped on shore without water. Other sea life awaits an uncertain fate in small pools of water left behind by the receding tide. These small pools—called tide pools—are home to a variety of sea life, including seaweed, sea anemones, sea stars, crabs, and clams. Each day, these creatures struggle for life in the pools, awaiting the next high tide.

At high tide, cool water fills the tide pools. The ocean water is full of oxygen and tiny creatures called plankton. Sea anemones, clams, and other animals feed on the tiny plankton. At low tide, the creatures are in danger of using up all the oxygen and food in the pool. In addition, the water in the pool gets warm and begins to dry up. Some creatures do not survive. Some animals, such as sea anemones and clams, close up to keep from losing water. Some seaweed secretes mucus that helps to keep it moist. When the waves finally reach high tide again, the pools are flooded with cool, rich seawater. What at first seems like a moment of relief becomes another struggle to again avoid being carried to shore by the waves.

Reading Time _____

Recalling Facts

1. At high tide, some forms of sea life, such as sea snails and seaweed, cling to rocks to avoid being
   - ❑ a. eaten by fish.
   - ❑ b. carried to shore by waves.
   - ❑ c. covered by water.

2. As water in a tide pool dries up, sea anemones and clams close up to keep from
   - ❑ a. losing water.
   - ❑ b. drowning.
   - ❑ c. getting cold.

3. Seaweed secretes mucus that helps to
   - ❑ a. keep flies off it.
   - ❑ b. keep waves from hitting it.
   - ❑ c. keep it moist.

4. While awaiting high tide, creatures in a tide pool are in danger of
   - ❑ a. getting cold.
   - ❑ b. using up all the food in the pool.
   - ❑ c. drowning.

5. Cool seawater pours into tide pools at
   - ❑ a. high tide.
   - ❑ b. low tide.
   - ❑ c. all times of the day.

Understanding Ideas

6. It is possible to conclude from the article that high tide occurs about
   - ❑ a. every hour.
   - ❑ b. twice a day.
   - ❑ c. once a week.

7. The article suggests that at high tide, some forms of sea life struggle to
   - ❑ a. keep from being covered in water.
   - ❑ b. get enough oxygen.
   - ❑ c. avoid being washed up on shore.

8. The article suggests that at low tide, sea life in tide pools struggles to
   - ❑ a. get enough food and moisture.
   - ❑ b. protect itself from crashing waves.
   - ❑ c. escape large deep-water enemies like sharks.

9. The article teaches us that sea creatures at the seashore have many traits that help them to survive in
   - ❑ a. a polluted environment.
   - ❑ b. changing conditions.
   - ❑ c. bad weather.

10. It is possible to infer from the article that the animals most successful at surviving in tide pools can
    - ❑ a. survive by eating only seaweed.
    - ❑ b. obtain oxygen from the air.
    - ❑ c. live out of water for hours at a time.

Getting the Salt out of Salt Water

A person adrift at sea cannot survive without freshwater. Drinking salt water only makes a person thirstier. Is there a way to change salt water to pure water to make it drinkable?

In this experiment, you will try to change salt water to freshwater. Though it takes only a few minutes to set up, the experiment will need to sit for a few hours. The materials needed are a clean tuna can, a clean wide-mouthed jar with a lid, salt, water, a measuring cup, and a spoon.

The first step is to add a fourth of a cup of salt to the tuna can. Be careful not to touch the sharp top edge of the can. Next, add a third of a cup of water to the can and stir. Once the salt is dissolved, carefully place the can inside the large jar. Cover it tightly and place it near a sunny window or heater. Let it sit there until the water has evaporated.

After a few hours, place the sealed jar in a refrigerator. The change in temperature will cause the water vapor to become liquid again. Once droplets have formed on the inside of the jar, open the jar and taste a droplet. If the droplet does not taste salty, the salt water has become freshwater.

1. **Recognizing Words in Context**

   Find the word *evaporated* in the passage. One definition below is closest to the meaning of that word. One definition has the opposite or nearly opposite meaning. The remaining definition has a completely different meaning. Label the definitions C for *closest*, O for *opposite or nearly opposite*, and D for *different*.

   _____ a. changed to liquid

   _____ b. changed to gas

   _____ c. changed color

2. **Distinguishing Fact from Opinion**

   Two of the statements below present *facts*, which can be proved correct. The other statement is an *opinion*, which expresses someone's thoughts or beliefs. Label the statements F for *fact* and O for *opinion*.

   _____ a. More ways are needed to change salt water to freshwater.

   _____ b. A person cannot survive without freshwater.

   _____ c. Heat causes water to become a vapor.

3. Keeping Events in Order

Label the statements below 1, 2, and 3 to show the order in which the steps should be performed.

_____ a. Place the jar in the refrigerator, allowing water droplets to form on the inside of the jar.

_____ b. Place the can of salt water inside the jar and put the lid on.

_____ c. Place the jar by a sunny window or near a heater.

4. Making Correct Inferences

Two of the statements below are correct *inferences,* or reasonable guesses. They are based on information in the passage. The other statement is an incorrect, or faulty, inference. Label the statements C for *correct* inference and F for *faulty* inference.

_____ a. Changing water to vapor and then bringing the water back again purifies the water.

_____ b. Freshwater cannot be changed into salt water.

_____ c. Drinking only salt water is harmful to humans.

5. Understanding Main Ideas

One of the statements below expresses the main idea of the passage. One statement is too general, or too broad. The other explains only part of the passage; it is too narrow. Label the statements M for *main idea,* B for *too broad,* and N for *too narrow.*

_____ a. Droplets form inside a sealed jar of water vapor when the jar is cooled.

_____ b. Salt can be removed from salt water by changing the water into vapor and then back to water again.

_____ c. There are a number of ways to get the salt out of salt water.

Correct Answers, Part A _____

Correct Answers, Part B _____

Total Correct Answers _____

The Invention of the Camera

It is the nature of invention that ideas develop over time. This was certainly true in the invention of the camera. A concept known to Greeks and Arabs a thousand or more years ago is basic to the camera. This concept is that during daytime, a tiny hole in the wall of an unlighted, windowless room projects an image from outside into the room.

About 500 years ago, this concept was used in the creation of an enclosed area with an opening that let in a beam of light. Artists used this "camera obscura" to project images onto paper. They then traced and painted the images. The enclosure worked in a way similar to a camera. What it lacked was a way to record an image automatically.

In the early 1800s, a man named Thomas Wedgwood coated a sheet of paper with a chemical that contained silver. He found that the paper could record an image when exposed to light but that it got darker and darker the longer that light shone on it. A French inventor named Joseph Niepce worked with this idea to make a paper to use in the camera obscura. Niepce was able to make a black-and-white image with his light-sensitive paper. With the use of an acid, he was also able to keep the image from turning black. There was a problem, though. The black areas and the white areas were reversed. Niepce had made the first negative.

Niepce began to work on a second method to make a print. In 1827 he used light-sensitive chemicals on a metal plate. Then he exposed the plate in a camera obscura all day. This faint image was the first photograph.

Later, Niepce shared his work with a French inventor named Louis Daguerre. Daguerre perfected a coating for the metal plate. A sharp image called a daguerreotype formed on the new plate in 20 minutes. After this advance, the first camera was made available for sale to the public in 1839. But creating a photograph was still a complex chemical process.

It wasn't until George Eastman invented the Kodak camera in 1888 that people had the first snapshot camera. It used roll film. For the first time, people did not have to fuss with chemicals to take a picture. Since then, the process has become even simpler. With the instant cameras and digital cameras of today, photos are available instantaneously.

Reading Time _____

Recalling Facts

1. The first photograph was made in 1827 by
   - ❑ a. Joseph Niepce.
   - ❑ b. ancient Greeks.
   - ❑ c. George Eastman.

2. With Daguerre's invention of a coated metal plate, an image formed
   - ❑ a. instantly.
   - ❑ b. in 20 minutes.
   - ❑ c. in 24 hours.

3. The Kodak camera invented by George Eastman was the first
   - ❑ a. camera.
   - ❑ b. snapshot camera.
   - ❑ c. camera sold to the public.

4. Pictures became available immediately with the invention of
   - ❑ a. lenses.
   - ❑ b. coated metal plates.
   - ❑ c. instant and digital cameras.

5. An enclosed area that worked like a camera but could not automatically record an image was the
   - ❑ a. daguerreotype.
   - ❑ b. camera obscura.
   - ❑ c. Kodak camera.

Understanding Ideas

6. It is possible to conclude from the article that a disadvantage of Niepce's first camera was the
   - ❑ a. length of time it took for an image to form.
   - ❑ b. amount of film used on one image.
   - ❑ c. large number of people needed to work the camera.

7. According to the article, light-sensitive papers and metal plates were needed to
   - ❑ a. measure temperature.
   - ❑ b. create enough light for picture taking.
   - ❑ c. record images in a camera.

8. You can infer that the invention of the camera is the result of
   - ❑ a. the ideas of just one person.
   - ❑ b. the work of many people over time.
   - ❑ c. an accident.

9. The article suggests that a disadvantage of the camera obscura was that there was
   - ❑ a. no way to automatically record an image.
   - ❑ b. no way to project images.
   - ❑ c. no lens.

10. The article suggests that people no longer had to fuss with chemicals to take pictures after the invention of
    - ❑ a. coated metal plates.
    - ❑ b. the camera obscura.
    - ❑ c. the snapshot camera.

Preparing for the Science Fair

The science fair was just a few weeks away, and Carla hadn't designed a project yet. She knew she wanted to do a photography project. She loved taking pictures. But what kind of project could she do with a camera?

At the library, Carla found a book that showed how to make a simple camera. Instead of a glass lens, the homemade camera had a pinhole. As light from the outside passed through the small hole, an image was projected inside the camera, just as with a camera obscura. The materials needed to make the camera were a cardboard canister, aluminum foil, black tape, scissors, and a needle.

Making the camera seemed simple, but taking pictures would be more involved. Carla would need to buy light-sensitive photo paper and find a darkroom to use. It was a good thing her mother worked for a small newspaper. Carla thought they had a darkroom she might be able to use.

Carla had an answer about the darkroom the next night. The project was a go! The newspaper photographer, Mr. Gomez, even offered to teach Carla how to develop her own prints. Carla set to work on the camera right away. She had a great deal of work to do. She would need to design a poster to explain how the camera worked. And, of course, she would need to take lots of pictures!

1. **Recognizing Words in Context**

   Find the word *involved* in the passage. One definition below is closest to the meaning of that word. One definition has the opposite or nearly opposite meaning. The remaining definition has a completely different meaning. Label the definitions C for *closest*, O for *opposite or nearly opposite*, and D for *different*.

   _____ a. easy

   _____ b. complicated

   _____ c. boring

2. **Distinguishing Fact from Opinion**

   Two of the statements below present *facts*, which can be proved correct. The other statement is an *opinion*, which expresses someone's thoughts or beliefs. Label the statements F for *fact* and O for *opinion*.

   _____ a. A pinhole acts as a lens in a simple camera.

   _____ b. Making a camera is an interesting project for a science fair.

   _____ c. Light passes through a small hole and projects an image inside the camera.

3. Keeping Events in Order

Label the statements below 1, 2, and 3 to show the order in which the events happened.

_____ a. Carla did not know what kind of project to do.

_____ b. Mr. Gomez offered to help.

_____ c. Carla needed to find a darkroom to develop pictures.

4. Making Correct Inferences

Two of the statements below are correct *inferences,* or reasonable guesses. They are based on information in the passage. The other statement is an incorrect, or faulty, inference. Label the statements C for *correct* inference and F for *faulty* inference.

_____ a. Carla is well prepared for the science fair.

_____ b. A simple camera can be made from household materials.

_____ c. Carla will win a prize at the science fair.

5. Understanding Main Ideas

One of the statements below expresses the main idea of the passage. One statement is too general, or too broad. The other explains only part of the passage; it is too narrow. Label the statements M for *main idea,* B for *too broad,* and N for *too narrow.*

_____ a. A pinhole camera can be made from household materials.

_____ b. Choosing a science fair project requires thought and research.

_____ c. A pinhole can function as a lens.

Correct Answers, Part A _____

Correct Answers, Part B _____

Total Correct Answers _____

A machine is a device that does work. In science, the word *work* is used to describe a force that acts on an object to move it. For example, carpenters do work when they pull nails out of wood. Movers do work when they load boxes onto a truck. They use simple machines to do these tasks.

Machines make it easier to do work because a person using them needs to use less force to move an object. Using the claw end of a hammer to pull nails out of wood requires less force than pulling the nails out with fingers. Pushing a heavy box up a ramp onto a truck requires less force than lifting the heavy box onto the truck.

The hammer and the ramp are examples of two types of simple machines. The hammer is an example of a lever, a bar that transfers force from one point to another while turning on a third point. A ramp is an example of a type of simple machine called an inclined plane. Besides levers and inclined planes, other types of simple machines include wedges, screws, wheels and axles, and pulleys.

When two or more simple machines are combined, they form a compound machine. For example, an ax is made up of two simple machines, the wedge and the lever. The blade of the ax is the wedge. It has a wide end and a thin, sharpened edge. The handle is a lever.

A wheelbarrow is a compound machine made up of a lever and a wheel and axle. The handles of the wheelbarrow act as levers to lift materials. Force applied to the wheel turns a shaft at the center of the wheel called an axle. This causes the wheelbarrow to move.

A bicycle is a compound machine that uses a variety of simple machines. Brake handles on a bicycle are levers. A screw connects the handlebars with the front wheel for steering. The wheels, pedals, and gears are all separate wheel and axle systems. These systems work together so that little force is required to make the bike move.

Imagine trying to chop wood without the wedge or lever of the ax. Imagine pushing a heavy load in a wheelbarrow without a wheel and axle. Using simple machines makes work easier to do. Combining simple machines to form compound machines, however, makes work easier still.

Reading Time _____

Recalling Facts

1. When two or more simple machines are combined, they form a
   - ❑ a. compound machine.
   - ❑ b. lever.
   - ❑ c. screw.

2. Levers, inclined planes, wedges, screws, wheels and axles, and pulleys are types of
   - ❑ a. ramps.
   - ❑ b. tools.
   - ❑ c. simple machines.

3. A compound machine made up of a lever and a wheel and axle is
   - ❑ a. a hammer.
   - ❑ b. a wheelbarrow.
   - ❑ c. an ax.

4. When a person uses a machine,
   - ❑ a. more concentration is needed.
   - ❑ b. doing work is more difficult.
   - ❑ c. doing work is easier.

5. There are _____ types of simple machines.
   - ❑ a. twelve
   - ❑ b. one
   - ❑ c. six

Understanding Ideas

6. A seesaw on a playground is an example of a
   - ❑ a. wheel and axle.
   - ❑ b. wedge.
   - ❑ c. lever.

7. The platform that leads from a pier to the deck of a ship is an example of a
   - ❑ a. complex machine.
   - ❑ b. simple machine.
   - ❑ c. compound machine.

8. It is possible to conclude that using a compound machine instead of a simple machine to complete a task makes the work _____ to do.
   - ❑ a. easier
   - ❑ b. harder
   - ❑ c. equally difficult

9. Machines make work easier to do because they
   - ❑ a. allow people to use less force.
   - ❑ b. can do work without any involvement from people.
   - ❑ c. are more skillful than people.

10. A compound machine that uses a screw, levers, and several wheel and axle systems is
    - ❑ a. a wheelbarrow.
    - ❑ b. an ax.
    - ❑ c. a bicycle.

Bicycles on the Move

The ancestor of the modern bicycle was the velocipede, invented in 1860s by Pierre Lallement, a French carriage maker. It had pedals and cranks attached to its front wheel, and it was the first human-powered vehicle to have lasting popularity. A few years later James Starley of England changed the design so that the front wheel was much larger than the rear wheel. Thomas Stevens rode one of these "high wheelers" across the United States, Europe, and Asia. The front wheel of his bike was 1.2 meters (4 feet) tall. High wheelers were faster than their predecessors, but they were dangerous because the rider sat above the high front wheel. In 1885 Starley's nephew created the rover, a safer bicycle with a smaller front wheel. Like bikes today, the rover had tires of equal size, pedals, a chain, and brakes. Despite this new design, cars soon became the most popular form of transportation.

Today, using a bicycle instead of a car to get around has its benefits. Riding a bike cuts down on traffic and pollution. It is less expensive than driving a car or taking a bus. In China and India, there are more bicycles than cars on the road. But elsewhere, there is still work to be done to promote the bicycle as a beneficial form of transportation.

1. Recognizing Words in Context

Find the word *predecessors* in the passage. One definition below is closest to the meaning of that word. One definition has the opposite or nearly opposite meaning. The remaining definition has a completely different meaning. Label the definitions C for *closest*, O for *opposite or nearly opposite*, and D for *different*.

_____ a. things that come after

_____ b. things that come before

_____ c. things that go

2. Distinguishing Fact from Opinion

Two of the statements below present *facts*, which can be proved correct. The other statement is an *opinion*, which expresses someone's thoughts or beliefs. Label the statements F for *fact* and O for *opinion*.

_____ a. In China and India, there are more bicycles on the streets than cars.

_____ b. Riding a bike is the best way to get around a city.

_____ c. The front wheel of the high wheeler was taller than the wheels of a modern bike.

3. **Keeping Events in Order**

   Label the statements below 1, 2, and 3 to show the order in which the events happened.

   _____ a. The high wheeler was invented.

   _____ b. The rover was invented.

   _____ c. The velocipede was invented.

4. **Making Correct Inferences**

   Two of the statements below are correct *inferences*, or reasonable guesses. They are based on information in the passage. The other statement is an incorrect, or faulty, inference. Label the statements C for *correct* inference and F for *faulty* inference.

   _____ a. Soon there will be more bicycles than cars on the road everywhere.

   _____ b. The design of the bicycle has improved over time.

   _____ c. Bicycles have some advantages over cars.

5. **Understanding Main Ideas**

   One of the statements below expresses the main idea of the passage. One statement is too general, or too broad. The other explains only part of the passage; it is too narrow. Label the statements M for *main idea*, B for *too broad*, and N for *too narrow*.

   _____ a. The rover was similar to modern bicycles.

   _____ b. The design of the bicycle has improved over time.

   _____ c. The bicycle is a common means of transportation.

Correct Answers, Part A _____

Correct Answers, Part B _____

Total Correct Answers _____

The Spectrum of Light

Although the light of the sun looks colorless, it is not. White light is made up of light of different colors. In the late 17th century, the English scientist Isaac Newton explained how and why white light could be split into colors. He realized that there are different kinds of light and that each kind of light has its own properties.

Some kinds of light can be seen, and some cannot. Light that can be seen is called visible light. Light, like other forms of energy, travels in waves. Different forms of light have waves of different lengths. *Wavelength* is a term that scientists use to describe how long or short waves are. Radio waves are a type of invisible light with a long wavelength, whereas visible light and X rays are types of light with shorter wavelengths. When different types of light are grouped in order of their wavelength, they form what is called a spectrum.

One way to show that white light is made up of different colors is to pass it through an angled piece of glass called a prism. All light bends as it passes through glass or water. A straw in a glass of water looks bent because the water bends the light bouncing off the straw. A prism bends light of different wavelengths at different angles. Because the colors of light have different wavelengths, each color is bent in a different direction. As white light passes through a prism, the different colors bend at different angles and split into the spectrum. Because of each color's wavelength, the colors of light are always split in the same order. The colors of the spectrum of visible light are red, orange, yellow, green, blue, indigo, and violet. Red light has a longer wavelength than violet light.

Isaac Newton designed an experiment to show that a prism does not add or subtract anything when light passes through it. He passed white light through a prism to split the light into its band of colors. Then Newton blocked all the colors of light except the ray of red light. He passed the ray of red light through a second prism. The ray of red light was bent as it passed through the prism, but its color did not change. With this experiment, Newton proved that the sun's light was truly made up of light of different colors.

Reading Time _____

Recalling Facts

1. A piece of glass used to split light into a band of colors is called a
   - ❑ a. mirror.
   - ❑ b. lens.
   - ❑ c. prism.

2. The band of colors that makes up light is called
   - ❑ a. the spectrum.
   - ❑ b. a wavelength.
   - ❑ c. an X ray.

3. The length of a wave of energy is called its
   - ❑ a. bandwidth.
   - ❑ b. wavelength.
   - ❑ c. stream length.

4. In the late 17th century, _____ realized that there are different kinds of light.
   - ❑ a. Isaac Newton
   - ❑ b. Albert Einstein
   - ❑ c. Aristotle

5. The colors of the spectrum are
   - ❑ a. brown, black, white, and gold.
   - ❑ b. pink, purple, tan, chartreuse, and maroon.
   - ❑ c. red, orange, yellow, green, blue, indigo, and violet.

Understanding Ideas

6. The article suggests that although the light of the sun looks colorless, it is made up of
   - ❑ a. pure red light.
   - ❑ b. different colors of light.
   - ❑ c. blue and yellow light.

7. It is possible to conclude from the article that orange light is a part of
   - ❑ a. radio waves.
   - ❑ b. X-ray light.
   - ❑ c. white light.

8. The article suggests that X rays, like other forms of energy, travel in
   - ❑ a. waves.
   - ❑ b. laser beams.
   - ❑ c. low-energy particles.

9. The article teaches us that as light passes through water or a piece of glass,
   - ❑ a. the light is bent.
   - ❑ b. nothing happens to the light.
   - ❑ c. the light disappears.

10. Newton's experiment showed that when white light passes through a prism, its appearance changes but its _____ does not.
    - ❑ a. color
    - ❑ b. form
    - ❑ c. angle

14 B Recipe for a Rainbow

To understand how rainbows form, it is helpful to think first about the times when rainbows can be seen. When the sky is completely clouded over, or when it is clear and dry, there are no rainbows to be seen. But something magical happens when it begins to rain while the sun is shining. All of a sudden, a rainbow's arc of colors appears in the sky.

Actually, the formation of a rainbow is not magic at all. In fact, the reason a rainbow forms is a key concept in the science of light. As light from the sun passes through raindrops in the sky, water refracts the light and splits it into a spectrum of colors. The colors in the spectrum always appear in the same order. They are red, orange, yellow, green, blue, indigo, and violet. At a distance, these colors of light look like an arc in the sky.

When the rain is light, two rainbows, called a double rainbow, may appear. The colors of the second rainbow are seen in reverse order. This makes the second rainbow look like a reflection of the first, but it is not. Really, the second rainbow forms when light passes through the bottoms of raindrops rather than the tops. All that is needed in nature's recipe for a rainbow is sunlight and drops of water.

1. **Recognizing Words in Context**

   Find the word *refracts* in the passage. One definition below is closest to the meaning of that word. One definition has the opposite or nearly opposite meaning. The remaining definition has a completely different meaning. Label the definitions C for *closest*, O for *opposite or nearly opposite*, and D for *different*.

   _____ a. bends

   _____ b. colors

   _____ c. straightens

2. **Distinguishing Fact from Opinion**

   Two of the statements below present *facts*, which can be proved correct. The other statement is an *opinion*, which expresses someone's thoughts or beliefs. Label the statements F for *fact* and O for *opinion*.

   _____ a. A rainbow forms as sunlight passes through raindrops.

   _____ b. A rainbow is one of nature's most beautiful creations.

   _____ c. Rainbows do not appear on clear, dry days.

3. **Keeping Events in Order**

Label the statements below 1, 2, and 3 to show the order in which the events happen.

_____ a. Part of the sky clears, and the sun comes out.

_____ b. It begins to rain on a cloudy day.

_____ c. A rainbow appears in the sky.

4. **Making Correct Inferences**

Two of the statements below are correct *inferences,* or reasonable guesses. They are based on information in the passage. The other statement is an incorrect, or faulty, inference. Label the statements C for *correct* inference and F for *faulty* inference.

_____ a. When a rainbow appears, a double rainbow usually appears soon afterward.

_____ b. The first rainbow in a double rainbow forms when light passes through the tops of raindrops.

_____ c. Rainbows do not appear without sunlight and water droplets.

5. **Understanding Main Ideas**

One of the statements below expresses the main idea of the passage. One statement is too general, or too broad. The other explains only part of the passage; it is too narrow. Label the statements M for *main idea,* B for *too broad,* and N for *too narrow.*

_____ a. Light from the sun is made up of light of different colors.

_____ b. A double rainbow forms when sunlight passes through both the tops and bottoms of raindrops.

_____ c. Sunlight passing through raindrops is split into a band of colors that appears as a rainbow in the sky.

Correct Answers, Part A _____

Correct Answers, Part B _____

Total Correct Answers _____

15   A   Recycling Can Reduce Pollution

Each year in the United States, the average family throws out about a ton of trash. Paper, plastics, glass, and cans make up more than half of the trash thrown away. Food waste makes up another third. People in the United States use about 90 million glass bottles and 46 million cans every day. Much of this glass and metal simply becomes garbage, but some will be recycled and made into new products.

Pollution caused by waste is a complex problem. Waste disposal companies bury most garbage in landfills. Many landfills are full, and land for new sites is hard to find in some areas. Over time, trash slowly dissolves into chemicals. Some of these chemicals are poisonous and can pollute water. Another way to dispose of trash is to burn it. At incineration plants, trash is burned to produce energy. Although this is a beneficial use of trash, some of the gas produced in the process pollutes the air.

To cut down on pollution caused by waste, people can restrict the amount of trash they produce. They can do this by "reducing, reusing, and recycling."

To reduce, people limit the amount of new goods they use. Ways to reduce include using both sides of a sheet of scratch paper and using cloth bags for shopping. Buying products made from recycled paper, plastic, or glass is another way to reduce.

To reuse, people can save bags, containers, clothing, books, and toys so that they can be used more than once. Plastic bags and containers can be washed and reused. Clothing, books, and toys can be passed on to others for their use instead of being thrown away.

To recycle, people can separate from their trash the materials that can be used again to make new products. Paper, cans, glass, and plastic can be recycled. The most inexpensive material to recycle is paper. In many communities, workers pick up recyclable goods directly from homes. People living in communities that do not have pickup service may need to bring their recyclables to a nearby recycling center.

Another way to recycle is to compost food waste. People can pile raw food waste outside in a wooden bin with straw or dead leaves. The food waste and plant matter break down and can be used to fertilize gardens. By recycling, reducing, and reusing the products we consume, we can cut down on trash and pollution.

Reading Time _____

Recalling Facts

1. Each year, an average family in the United States throws away about
   - ❏ a. half a ton of trash.
   - ❏ b. one ton of trash.
   - ❏ c. five tons of trash.

2. Most household trash is buried in areas called
   - ❏ a. landfills.
   - ❏ b. volcanoes.
   - ❏ c. wells.

3. The process in which goods are used again to make new products is called
   - ❏ a. disposal.
   - ❏ b. pollution.
   - ❏ c. recycling.

4. _____ is the least costly material to recycle.
   - ❏ a. Glass
   - ❏ b. Paper
   - ❏ c. Metal

5. One way to cut down on pollution caused by waste is to
   - ❏ a. reuse more goods.
   - ❏ b. build more landfills.
   - ❏ c. burn chemical waste.

Understanding Ideas

6. The article suggests that garbage disposal is a problem in the United States because
   - ❏ a. pollution is destroying many cities.
   - ❏ b. in some areas there are fewer and fewer place to put garbage.
   - ❏ c. so many people are recycling that there are not enough factories to handle the material.

7. You can infer that recycling decreases pollution by
   - ❏ a. reducing trash.
   - ❏ b. making more trash.
   - ❏ c. burning trash.

8. From the information in the article, you can infer that one problem that old landfills create is
   - ❏ a. taking up space that should be used for factories that produce glass.
   - ❏ b. causing more air pollution than automobiles.
   - ❏ c. leaking poisonous chemicals into underground water supplies.

9. If there was a large amount of spoiled food in the back of a refrigerator, what could a person do with it to help the waste problem?
   - ❏ a. Throw it in the garbage immediately.
   - ❏ b. Put it in a compost pile.
   - ❏ c. Take it to a recycling center.

10. It is possible to conclude from the article that _____ household waste is being thrown away.
    - ❏ a. too much
    - ❏ b. the right amount of
    - ❏ c. not enough

15 B   Fighting Air Pollution

More than a hundred years ago, large smokestacks were a common sight in city neighborhoods in the United States. Great amounts of smoke fouled the air and caused health problems. An inventor named Mary Walton wanted to decrease air pollution. She came up with a way to pass smoke through water tanks before it was released into the air. The water absorbed some of the pollutants, and then it was flushed into the sewers.

Like Walton, Frederick Cottrell knew that pollution from smokestacks needed to be controlled. He invented a device that took out more than 90 percent of the harmful particles found in smoke. The device used an electric current to pull bits of matter out of the smoke. The device was successful and became known as the Cottrell.

The fight against air pollution did not end with the Cottrell. During the 1970s and 1980s, the African-American inventor Meredith Gourdine adapted Cottrell's ideas for other uses. These included using electric current to remove pollutants in automobile exhaust systems and incinerator smokestacks. Gourdine also developed a device that helps to clear smoke from buildings during fires. The work of these inventors and others has helped to make the air less polluted.

1. **Recognizing Words in Context**

   Find the word *fouled* in the passage. One definition below is closest to the meaning of that word. One definition has the opposite or nearly opposite meaning. The remaining definition has a completely different meaning. Label the definitions C for *closest*, O for *opposite or nearly opposite*, and D for *different*.

   _____ a. made dirty

   _____ b. made illegal

   _____ c. made clean

2. **Distinguishing Fact from Opinion**

   Two of the statements below present *facts*, which can be proved correct. The other statement is an *opinion*, which expresses someone's thoughts or beliefs. Label the statements F for *fact* and O for *opinion*.

   _____ a. Mary Walton worked to decrease air pollution.

   _____ b. One of Gourdine's inventions helps clear smoke during fires.

   _____ c. Inventions that reduce air pollution are extremely valuable.

3. Keeping Events in Order

Label the statements below 1, 2, and 3 to show the order in which the events happened.

_____ a. Mary Walton invented a device that flushes pollutants away with sewage.

_____ b. Meredith Gourdine invented a way to reduce pollutants in car exhaust.

_____ c. Frederick Cottrell invented a device that takes out more than 90 percent of the harmful particles found in smoke.

4. Making Correct Inferences

Two of the statements below are correct *inferences*, or reasonable guesses. They are based on information in the passage. The other statement is an incorrect, or faulty, inference. Label the statements C for *correct* inference and F for *faulty* inference.

_____ a. Taking harmful bits of matter out of smoke is a key to reducing air pollution.

_____ b. Cottrell's use of electric current to remove pollutants has led to many other inventions.

_____ c. The work of these three inventors has done more to clean up the air than anyone else's has.

5. Understanding Main Ideas

One of the statements below expresses the main idea of the passage. One statement is too general, or too broad. The other explains only part of the passage; it is too narrow. Label the statements M for *main idea*, B for *too broad*, and N for *too narrow.*

_____ a. Air pollution is caused by smoke and harmful chemicals that enter the air.

_____ b. Frederick Cottrell developed an important method of cleaning smoke.

_____ c. Inventions have been helpful in the fight against air pollution.

Correct Answers, Part A _____

Correct Answers, Part B _____

Total Correct Answers _____

72

For many centuries, people were not able to explore most parts of the underwater world. They were limited by two things: lack of air and the tremendous amount of pressure deep in the sea. Even the best divers could hold their breath underwater for only two or three minutes, and they could dive little more than 10 meters (33 feet) below the surface.

To learn more about the ocean world, people needed a way to breathe underwater. Records from ancient civilizations show that divers used tubes and pipes to breathe air from the surface while underwater. But they still could not dive very deep.

In more recent times, people have created diving equipment to try to solve these problems. In the 16th century, divers tried to use a tight helmet with a long leather breathing tube. The tube was attached to a container of air on the surface, but there was no way for fresh air to enter the container. Used air filled the helmet and could cause a diver to suffocate. Some inventors designed diving bells, which were upside-down containers that held air underwater. Divers could go into the diving bell when they needed to take a few breaths, but after a while the oxygen would run out.

In the 1830s in London, Augustus Siebe created a diving suit with a metal helmet and metal chest covering. Air from the surface was pumped through a pipe into the helmet. With this suit, a diver could reach 60 meters (200 feet) below the surface. The metal suit kept the body safe from the pressure of the water at this depth. With modern armored suits, divers can go 400 meters (1,300 feet) underwater. Scuba gear designed by Jacques Cousteau and Emile Gagnan allowed divers to carry air tanks on their backs. Divers could spend more time underwater and move with ease.

A new age of technology gave rise to undersea chambers and vehicles. Chambers could be lowered from boats to depths of 1 kilometer (3,200 feet). Such vehicles as bathyscaphes and submersibles have been used to study the depths of the sea. In 1960, Jacques Picard piloted a bathyscaphe called the *Trieste* to the deepest part of the ocean. These days, remote-controlled vehicles are used to explore the ocean depths. These machines can record data and collect samples. Each of these new designs has allowed humans to further explore the undersea world.

Reading Time _____

Recalling Facts

1. Tubes and pipes from the surface allowed early divers to
   - ❑ a. protect themselves from water pressure.
   - ❑ b. swim faster than ever before.
   - ❑ c. breathe underwater.

2. The first diving suits did not allow divers to
   - ❑ a. stay underwater longer.
   - ❑ b. rise to the surface.
   - ❑ c. breathe fresh air for very long.

3. Diving suits that protected the body from water pressure were made of
   - ❑ a. metal or armor.
   - ❑ b. cloth.
   - ❑ c. leather.

4. The deepest part of the ocean
   - ❑ a. has never been reached by humans.
   - ❑ b. has been reached by a diver in scuba gear.
   - ❑ c. has been reached by humans in undersea vehicles.

5. An invention by Jacques Cousteau and Emile Gagnan that allowed divers to carry air tanks is called
   - ❑ a. scuba gear.
   - ❑ b. the diving bell.
   - ❑ c. the *Trieste*.

Understanding Ideas

6. From the article, it is possible to conclude that a device that allows humans to breathe underwater for a long period of time is
   - ❑ a. scuba gear.
   - ❑ b. a remote-controlled vehicle.
   - ❑ c. metal armor.

7. It is possible to conclude that a device that protects the body from water pressure is
   - ❑ a. a leather breathing tube.
   - ❑ b. scuba gear.
   - ❑ c. an armored diving suit.

8. The article suggests that the invention of underwater gear has
   - ❑ a. allowed humans to explore the ocean.
   - ❑ b. prevented humans from exploring the ocean.
   - ❑ c. had no effect on human study of the ocean.

9. A likely reason that samples of rock from the ocean floor are helpful to scientists would be that
   - ❑ a. the samples might reveal clues about the history of Earth.
   - ❑ b. valuable minerals are easily found on the ocean floor.
   - ❑ c. the ocean floor is covered with meteorites.

10. The word *scuba* is actually an acronym. What words might *scuba* likely stand for?
    - ❑ a. swimmers combining unusual breathing activities
    - ❑ b. self-contained underwater breathing apparatus
    - ❑ c. sinking can undo bathyscaphe activity

Snorkeling is a way to explore the undersea world without having to wear a lot of diving equipment. All that a person needs is a snorkel, a mask, and flippers. A snorkeler—a person who snorkels—can enjoy the bright colors of fish and coral in shallow waters.

The snorkel is a tube that extends above the surface of the water when a snorkeler is floating face down on the surface. The snorkel allows the snorkeler to breathe air. A mouthpiece is connected to the tube and fits snugly between a diver's lips and teeth. A diver can float facedown in the water taking in all the sights while breathing through the snorkel. The snorkel is attached to the mask to help keep the open end of the tube above water.

The mask allows the diver to see clearly while underwater. The mask, held on by a strap around the head, forms a tight seal over the eyes and nose so that water does not enter. By covering the nose, masks make divers breathe through their mouths.

Diving below the surface with a snorkel is not a problem. Snorkelers hold their breath and use the flippers to kick below the surface to get a closer look at fish and coral. When air is needed, the snorkeler returns to the surface and clears water out of the snorkel by exhaling strongly.

1. **Recognizing Words in Context**

   Find the word *snugly* in the passage. One definition below is closest to the meaning of that word. One definition has the opposite or nearly opposite meaning. The remaining definition has a completely different meaning. Label the definitions C for *closest*, O for *opposite or nearly opposite*, and D for *different*.

   _____ a. loosely

   _____ b. sleepily

   _____ c. tightly

2. **Distinguishing Fact from Opinion**

   Two of the statements below present *facts*, which can be proved correct. The other statement is an *opinion*, which expresses someone's thoughts or beliefs. Label the statements F for *fact* and O for *opinion*.

   _____ a. Snorkeling is a fun and easy way to explore the undersea world.

   _____ b. A snorkel allows a person to breathe while floating in water.

   _____ c. The mask forms a tight seal over the eyes and nose.

3. Keeping Events in Order

Label the statements below 1, 2, and 3 to show the order in which the events happen.

_____ a. The divers can once again view the undersea world while breathing with ease.

_____ b. To clear water out of the snorkel at the surface, snorkelers exhale strongly.

_____ c. Snorkelers hold their breath and use their flippers to swim below the surface.

4. Making Correct Inferences

Two of the statements below are correct *inferences,* or reasonable guesses. They are based on information in the passage. The other statement is an incorrect, or faulty, inference. Label the statements C for *correct* inference and F for *faulty* inference.

_____ a. To snorkel, a person needs to know how to swim.

_____ b. With a snorkel, a person can dive deep below the surface for as long as 30 minutes.

_____ c. With a snorkel, a diver can look deeper into the water than a person on a boat can.

5. Understanding Main Ideas

One of the statements below expresses the main idea of the passage. One statement is too general, or too broad. The other explains only part of the passage; it is too narrow. Label the statements M for *main idea,* B for *too broad,* and N for *too narrow.*

_____ a. Snorkeling equipment allows a person to explore shallow waters.

_____ b. People use snorkeling equipment to explore the undersea world.

_____ c. A snorkel consists of a tube and a mouthpiece.

Correct Answers, Part A _____

Correct Answers, Part B _____

Total Correct Answers _____

The Endangered Everglades

Everglades National Park in Florida is home to a wide array of life. A grassy river of slow-moving water is the source of life for plants and animals of this region. Water flows more than 160 kilometers (100 miles) from Lake Okeechobee to marshes at the sea. Within the river, island forests are home to trees, plants, and animals. Other trees, such as cypress and mangrove, grow right in the water. Birds nest in the trees or wade among them, feeding on shrimp and fish.

Within Everglades National Park are a number of endangered species. Among the endangered plants is the Garber's spurge, one of more than 1,000 kinds of plants that grow in the park. The American crocodile, the wood stork, and the Florida panther are just a few of the endangered animals that live in the park. Not only plants and animals in the Everglades are in danger—the Everglades region itself is in danger of dying out. The Everglades' status as a national park has not been enough to protect it from environmental changes.

The balance of nature in the Everglades has changed a great deal because of the way people in Florida have used water. Some developers have drained wetlands to build new homes and roads. Some of the water that once flowed through the Everglades is now used by homes and farms. Less water flowing through the park means less food for endangered birds such as the wood stork and the snail kite.

The Everglades also has a dry season. This season is an important feeding time for some animals. As the river dries up into pools, fish and other food sources become concentrated in small areas, making them easy prey for predators. But there are occasional rainstorms during this season, and urban areas release excess water into the Everglades to prevent their streets from flooding. This refills the river and disturbs the food supply for Everglades predators. It also washes away bird, crocodile, and alligator eggs. Some of these animals are endangered species.

In the fight to save life and the park itself, the federal government has added new land to the park. The land gives animals more room to find food and to nest, but it does not solve the water problem. To do this, people will have to work together to protect the Everglades through better management of Florida's water resources.

Reading Time _____

Recalling Facts

1. The source of life for plants and animals in the Everglades is a
   - ❏ a. large pine forest.
   - ❏ b. grassy river.
   - ❏ c. glacier.

2. The American crocodile, the wood stork, and the Florida panther are
   - ❏ a. endangered animals of the Everglades.
   - ❏ b. living in large numbers in the Everglades.
   - ❏ c. creatures that no longer live in the Everglades.

3. The balance of nature in the Everglades has changed a great deal because of
   - ❏ a. very cold temperatures.
   - ❏ b. a lack of rain.
   - ❏ c. the way people use water in the region.

4. New land added to the park has
   - ❏ a. solved all the problems in the Everglades.
   - ❏ b. solved the water problem in the Everglades.
   - ❏ c. given animals more room to find food and to nest.

5. Garber's spurge is one of more than 1,000 kinds of _____ found in Everglades National Park.
   - ❏ a. insects
   - ❏ b. fish
   - ❏ c. plants

Understanding Ideas

6. It is possible to conclude from the article that without water, life in the Everglades
   - ❏ a. would not survive.
   - ❏ b. would thrive.
   - ❏ c. would not change.

7. The article suggests that more water flowing through the park in the dry season
   - ❏ a. helps the animals.
   - ❏ b. harms the animals.
   - ❏ c. does not affect the animals.

8. From the article, it is possible to conclude that to solve the water problem in the Everglades, people need to
   - ❏ a. stop using water.
   - ❏ b. close the national park.
   - ❏ c. work together to protect nature and still meet human needs for water.

9. From the article, it is possible to conclude that a visitor to Everglades National Park is likely to see
   - ❏ a. a snow-covered mountain peak.
   - ❏ b. tall grass and trees growing in shallow water.
   - ❏ c. cacti.

10. The article suggests that protected lands can be
    - ❏ a. harmed by what happens outside of them.
    - ❏ b. harmful to places around them.
    - ❏ c. kept safe from any harm.

The purpose of U.S. national parks has changed over the years. In the early years, the main purpose of the parks was to give people a chance to enjoy the beauty of nature. Protecting wild animals in the parks was not a high priority. In fact, feeding bears was allowed so that people might see them up close. Today, park rangers know how unsafe this is for people and how harmful this is to bears. Bears that come to depend on food from humans cannot exist in the wild. They can cause much damage to property if food from humans is not easy to find.

Since 1916, one of the missions of the national parks has been to protect wild animals. Parks are often the only wild habitats, or natural homes, left for endangered animals. For example, Kentucky cave shrimp live only in and near Mammoth Cave National Park. Rangers there study the shrimp and their habitat to learn how to best protect them.

Before national parks became protected places for animals, some groups of animals were harmed there. Today, animals that had disappeared from their park habitats are being restored. Wolf packs that once roamed Yellowstone National Park have been brought back. In the early years of the park, many wolves in the region were killed. Today, park rangers monitor the new wolf packs to make sure they do well in their new park home.

1. **Recognizing Words in Context**

    Find the word *restored* in the passage. One definition below is closest to the meaning of that word. One definition has the opposite or nearly opposite meaning. The remaining definition has a completely different meaning. Label the definitions C for *closest*, O for *opposite or nearly opposite*, and D for *different*.

    _____ a. removed

    _____ b. shopped

    _____ c. returned

2. **Distinguishing Fact from Opinion**

    Two of the statements below present *facts*, which can be proved correct. The other statement is an *opinion*, which expresses someone's thoughts or beliefs. Label the statements F for *fact* and O for *opinion*.

    _____ a. Park rangers do a good job of protecting wild animals.

    _____ b. Today, one of the missions of the national parks is to protect wild animals.

    _____ c. Kentucky cave shrimp live only in and near Mammoth Cave National Park.

3. Keeping Events in Order

Two of the statements below describe events that happened at the same time. The other statement describes an event that happened before or after those events. Label them S for *same time*, B for *before*, and A for *after*.

_____ a. Many of the wolves in and around Yellowstone National Park were killed.

_____ b. Park rangers began to study park animals to learn how to best protect them.

_____ c. People were allowed to feed bears in national parks.

4. Making Correct Inferences

Two of the statements below are correct *inferences,* or reasonable guesses. They are based on information in the passage. The other statement is an incorrect, or faulty, inference. Label the statements C for *correct* inference and F for *faulty* inference.

_____ a. Wild animals that live in national parks are safe from being harmed by humans.

_____ b. Workers in national parks try to protect endangered animals and their homes.

_____ c. Some species of animals that once faced extinction now have a better chance of surviving.

5. Understanding Main Ideas

One of the statements below expresses the main idea of the passage. One statement is too general, or too broad. The other explains only part of the passage; it is too narrow. Label the statements M for *main idea*, B for *too broad*, and N for *too narrow*.

_____ a. The lives of wild animals are affected by people in many ways.

_____ b. Wolf packs are being brought back to Yosemite National Park.

_____ c. Protecting wild animals was not always a priority at national parks, but it is now.

Correct Answers, Part A _____

Correct Answers, Part B _____

Total Correct Answers _____

A Meal of Wild Forest Plants

Many wild plants found throughout the United States are edible; that is, they can be eaten. The part of the plant that can be eaten depends on the type of plant. Some plants have roots that are edible. Other edible plant parts include the stems, leaves, seeds, or even flowers. Edible plants grow at different times of the year and in different places. A menu for an autumn meal of forest plants could be watercress salad, arrowhead soup, acorn bread, and gooseberry pie. Watercress leaves, arrowhead roots, acorns, and gooseberries will need to be gathered for the meal.

Watercress grows in wet places such as springs or the edges of rivers. To find this plant, a person should look for masses of clover-like leaves on reddish stalks growing sideways in water. The roots of the plant and the small four-petal flowers are white. Watercress can be eaten raw in a salad or steamed like spinach.

When gathering arrowhead roots, a person should wear old clothes—this is a dirty job. The arrowhead plant grows in mud near ponds and rivers. A person looking for arrowhead plants should watch for a plant with arrow-shaped leaves and three white flowers on a single stalk. In the fall, the roots of this plant grow potato-like tubers that are tasty in soups with wild onions. Arrowhead tubers grow about 30 centimeters (12 inches) below the ground and about 1 meter (3¼ feet) from the stalk of the plant. A rake or shovel can be used to find them in the mud.

In the early autumn, acorns fall from oak trees. A substance called tannin makes the acorns bitter. Shelled acorns need to be soaked in water for a few days or boiled a few times to remove the tannin. When the acorns are no longer bitter, they can be baked and ground to make flour for bread.

Gooseberries grow in open areas of the forest. Gooseberries are small, round, and red. They grow on thorny shrubs and ripen in the autumn. To be sure that a shrub is in fact a gooseberry shrub, look for thorns and hand-shaped leaves with three or five fingers. The berries of the gooseberry shrub can be baked in a pie.

Only experts should gather wild plants for meals. Some poisonous wild plants resemble edible plants, and eating the wrong plant can cause serious illness or even death.

Reading Time _____

Recalling Facts

1. Edible plants are plants that
   - ❑ a. can be eaten.
   - ❑ b. cannot be eaten.
   - ❑ c. are poisonous.

2. An edible plant that grows in springs or along rivers is
   - ❑ a. a cactus.
   - ❑ b. an apple.
   - ❑ c. watercress.

3. An edible potato-like tuber that grows in the mud is
   - ❑ a. a gooseberry.
   - ❑ b. an arrowhead root.
   - ❑ c. a pumpkin.

4. Oak trees produce
   - ❑ a. acorns.
   - ❑ b. arrowhead roots.
   - ❑ c. pine nuts.

5. Small, round, red berries called gooseberries grow
   - ❑ a. on large thornless trees.
   - ❑ b. on thorny shrubs.
   - ❑ c. on underwater stalks without leaves.

Understanding Ideas

6. From information in the article, you can infer that a tuber is a
   - ❑ a. tall stalk.
   - ❑ b. large leaf.
   - ❑ c. thick root part.

7. To locate an edible plant, it is important to know where the plant grows and
   - ❑ a. what it looks like.
   - ❑ b. how it tastes.
   - ❑ c. how it is cooked.

8. Because of the bitter tannin in acorns, you can infer that the nut
   - ❑ a. must never be eaten.
   - ❑ b. must be handled carefully.
   - ❑ c. must always be soaked or boiled before eating.

9. It is likely that a person living in the wild who knew about edible plants
   - ❑ a. would go hungry.
   - ❑ b. would have a variety of plants to eat all year.
   - ❑ c. would have few plants to eat in only a few seasons of the year.

10. It is possible to conclude from the article that preparing an entire meal of wild plants
    - ❑ a. is not possible.
    - ❑ b. is possible if you know what to look for.
    - ❑ c. is dangerous.

18	B	The Origin of Corn

More than 70 countries produce corn, and the total amount they produce each year is more than 500 million tons. There are many varieties of corn. Corn is used as food for both animals and people. People use corn to make bread, tortillas, and cereals. It is also eaten as corn on the cob and popcorn. Corn is so widespread and diverse that scientists have found it difficult to understand how, where, and when corn evolved.

Plant scientists called botanists study plants to find the origin of corn. They look for wild plants that have existed for thousands of years and are similar to corn. In 1948, a college student found an ear of corn that was more than 5,000 years old. A group of researchers once found 23,000 ancient corn cobs. These samples of ancient corn help scientists to learn how corn came to be.

Most people agree that corn evolved in some way from a Mexican grass called teosinte. In 1976, Rafael Guzman discovered an ancient form of this grass. Scientists studied the grass to learn how it is like corn.

In spite of the record of ancient corn and teosinte, scientists are not sure how modern corn evolved. Some believe that corn is a direct descendant of the ancient grass, whereas others think there may have been an intermediate form of corn similar to the corn that is used for popcorn.

1. **Recognizing Words in Context**

Find the word *intermediate* in the passage. One definition below is closest to the meaning of that word. One definition has the opposite or nearly opposite meaning. The remaining definition has a completely different meaning. Label the definitions C for *closest*, O for *opposite or nearly opposite*, and D for *different*.

_____ a. in the middle

_____ b. at the end

_____ c. in a large amount

2. **Distinguishing Fact from Opinion**

Two of the statements below present *facts*, which can be proved correct. The other statement is an *opinion*, which expresses someone's thoughts or beliefs. Label the statements F for *fact* and O for *opinion*.

_____ a. Animals and people eat corn.

_____ b. Many scientists believe corn developed from an ancient grass.

_____ c. The best-tasting corn is corn on the cob.

3. Keeping Events in Order

Label the statements below 1, 2, and 3 to show the order in which the events happened.

_____ a. Some of the ancient teosinte plants began to develop into other plants.

_____ b. Modern corn appeared on Earth.

_____ c. An ancient form of teosinte appeared on Earth.

4. Making Correct Inferences

Two of the statements below are correct *inferences,* or reasonable guesses. They are based on information in the passage. The other statement is an incorrect, or faulty, inference. Label the statements C for *correct* inference and F for *faulty* inference.

_____ a. The origin of corn is not yet fully understood.

_____ b. Research and records of ancient wild plants help scientists learn about corn.

_____ c. Teosinte and modern corn are almost exactly the same.

5. Understanding Main Ideas

One of the statements below expresses the main idea of the passage. One statement is too general, or too broad. The other explains only part of the passage; it is too narrow. Label the statements M for *main idea,* B for *too broad,* and N for *too narrow.*

_____ a. Scientists study how wild plants became plants grown on farms.

_____ b. Scientists have been researching ancient plants to learn how corn came into being.

_____ c. Corn appears to have evolved from a Mexican grass.

Correct Answers, Part A _____

Correct Answers, Part B _____

Total Correct Answers _____

The human ear is able to hear a variety of sounds. The thud of a heavy object dropping to the ground, the soft hum of a fan, and the shrill ring of a bell are just a few of the different sounds that can be heard. To understand why there are so many different sounds, one needs to know what sound is.

Sound is a form of energy that travels in waves called sound waves, or acoustic waves. When an object moves quickly, it may produce sound waves. As the object vibrates, molecules of air are pushed together and then pulled apart. This action makes a wave of sound that travels through the air. The vibrations that create sound waves can be seen when a guitar string is plucked. They can also be felt by placing one's fingers on one's throat when speaking.

The speed of the vibration of the object sets the pitch of the sound that is made. A fast vibration forms short waves that produce a sound with a high pitch, such as a shrill bell or the screech of brakes. A slow vibration forms long waves that produce a sound with a low pitch, such as the thud of a heavy object striking the floor.

The strength of the vibration of the object determines how loud a sound is. A strong vibration makes big waves, and a weak vibration makes small waves. When a guitar string is plucked gently, the string vibrates weakly, and the sound is soft. When the string is plucked forcefully, the vibration is strong, and the sound is loud. How loud or soft a sound is can be measured in units called decibels.

To hear sound, humans and many animals have ears. The shape of the human ear helps the ear to gather sound waves and funnel them through a tube to the eardrum. As the waves pass through the eardrum, they cause it to vibrate. The body changes the vibrations into nerve impulses, which travel to the brain so that sense can be made of the sounds.

Not all sounds can be heard by humans. High-pitched sounds called ultrasound can be heard only by certain animals. Bats, dolphins, and whales depend on ultrasound to find food. With all of the sounds that are heard by humans, it may seem difficult to imagine that there are many others that cannot be heard.

Reading Time _____

Recalling Facts

1. Sound is a form of energy that travels in
   - ❑ a. sound routes.
   - ❑ b. sound packets.
   - ❑ c. sound waves.

2. The pitch of a sound is determined by the
   - ❑ a. speed of the vibration of an object.
   - ❑ b. size of the noise.
   - ❑ c. distance to the ear.

3. The strength of the vibration that makes a sound determines
   - ❑ a. how fast the sound moves.
   - ❑ b. how loud the sound is.
   - ❑ c. how deep the sound is.

4. The unit that measures loudness is the
   - ❑ a. wavelength.
   - ❑ b. amplifier.
   - ❑ c. decibel.

5. A kind of high-pitched sound heard only by certain animals is called
   - ❑ a. ultrasound.
   - ❑ b. a shriek.
   - ❑ c. a radio wave.

Understanding Ideas

6. Because air molecules are needed to produce sound, it is likely that in a place with no air, such as outer space,
   - ❑ a. only certain animals could hear sound.
   - ❑ b. sound is the same as it is on Earth.
   - ❑ c. there is no sound.

7. The article suggests that human beings hear
   - ❑ a. very few sounds.
   - ❑ b. many kinds of sounds.
   - ❑ c. every kind of sound.

8. The article suggests that ultrasound is a kind of sound heard
   - ❑ a. by all living things.
   - ❑ b. only by humans.
   - ❑ c. by some living things.

9. From the information in the article, you can infer that the high whistle of a teapot is made up of
   - ❑ a. long waves.
   - ❑ b. short waves.
   - ❑ c. medium-length waves.

10. An electric bass guitar with the volume turned up would have
   - ❑ a. a strong vibration.
   - ❑ b. a weak vibration.
   - ❑ c. no vibration.

Pleasant and Unpleasant Sounds

When a radio is on, most people will choose to listen to music rather than static. The reason for this is the difference between musical sounds and noise. There are some sounds that are pleasant to listen to and other sounds that are grating. A musical sound has a regular pattern of sound waves. In contrast, most noise is sound with no regular pattern.

Engineers have found a way to make some noises less irritating. First they measure the sound wave pattern of a noise. Then they produce a second sound with a wave pattern that is nearly the reverse of parts of the noise's wave pattern. When the two wave patterns meet, they overlap and cancel each other out. Hospitals have used this method in body scanners to make the machine quieter for patients. There is not much that can be done, however, to eliminate the noise of a jackhammer if you happen to be standing next to one.

Not all noise is unpleasant. Some noise, called white noise, can be relaxing. Like a waterfall, white noise consists of sound waves of all pitches. People who feel uncomfortable when it is completely silent in their homes can use machines that make white noise. Many companies have white noise in their offices because people seem to work better with white noise than they do when it is silent. In the end, what sounds are noise is personal opinion. What is a pleasant sound to one person may be noise to another.

1. **Recognizing Words in Context**

   Find the word *grating* in the passage. One definition below is closest to the meaning of that word. One definition has the opposite or nearly opposite meaning. The remaining definition has a completely different meaning. Label the definitions C for *closest,* O for *opposite or nearly opposite,* and D for *different.*

   _____ a. annoying

   _____ b. pleasant

   _____ c. loud

2. **Distinguishing Fact from Opinion**

   Two of the statements below present *facts,* which can be proved correct. The other statement is an *opinion,* which expresses someone's thoughts or beliefs. Label the statements F for *fact* and O for *opinion.*

   _____ a. A musical sound has a regular pattern.

   _____ b. White noise consists of sound waves of all pitches.

   _____ c. Silence is annoying, and white noise is peaceful.

3. **Keeping Events in Order**

   Label the statements below 1, 2, and 3 to show the order in which the events happen.

   _____ a. When the wave patterns meet, they cancel each other out, and little or no noise is heard.

   _____ b. To eliminate noise, engineers study the wave pattern of the noise.

   _____ c. A second wave pattern is produced that is nearly the reverse of the first.

4. **Making Correct Inferences**

   Two of the statements below are correct *inferences,* or reasonable guesses. They are based on information in the passage. The other statement is an incorrect, or faulty, inference. Label the statements C for *correct* inference and F for *faulty* inference.

   _____ a. The sound of a well-played violin has a regular wave pattern.

   _____ b. All noise is unpleasant to listen to.

   _____ c. A sound that is a pleasant to one person may be just noise to someone else.

5. **Understanding Main Ideas**

   One of the statements below expresses the main idea of the passage. One statement is too general, or too broad. The other explains only part of the passage; it is too narrow. Label the statements M for *main idea,* B for *too broad,* and N for *too narrow.*

   _____ a. Noise is a sound with no regular pattern that is often unpleasant to listen to.

   _____ b. Engineers can reduce or eliminate unpleasant noise.

   _____ c. Forms of energy that travel in waves include light and sound.

Correct Answers, Part A _____

Correct Answers, Part B _____

Total Correct Answers _____

Climate and the Change of Seasons

In some parts of the United States, the weather changes drastically during the year. Cold and snowy winters give way to hot and humid summers. In other parts of the country, it is warm year-round. In the tropics, near the equator, it is always hot. At the poles, it is always cold, even in the summer when the sun shines for up to 24 hours a day. The most important reason for these differences in climate is the tilt of Earth's axis as Earth orbits the Sun.

Earth's axis is the imaginary line that runs through the middle of Earth, from the North Pole to the South Pole. For half of the year, or half of Earth's orbit, the northern half of Earth tilts toward the Sun. For the other half of the year, the southern half of Earth tilts toward the Sun. More direct light and heat reach the half of Earth that is tilted toward the Sun, making it warmer on that half. At that time the season is summer. The half of Earth tilted away from the Sun receives less direct heat and light. The season in that half of the world is winter. Summer starts in June in the northern half of the world, and summer starts in December in the southern half of the world.

The angle of the Sun changes little in the tropics along the equator. This region receives direct sunlight year-round and is always hot. Instead of summer and winter, the tropics may have a dry or a wet season based on the amount of rainfall.

The angle of the Sun at the North Pole and South Pole makes these places cold. In the summer, when a pole is tilted toward the Sun, the Sun may shine up to 24 hours a day. The angle of the rays is so sharp, however, that the heat of the rays is very weak. In the winter, when the pole is tilted away from the Sun, the rays of the Sun hit the pole for only a few hours a day or sometimes not at all. Winters at the poles are dark and bitterly cold. Without the summer months in these or other cold regions, it is doubtful that life could survive. The length and warmth of the summer in any particular part of the world helps determine what kinds of plants and animals live there.

Reading Time _____

Recalling Facts

1. The differences in Earth's climates and seasons are explained by
   - ❏ a. the tilt of Earth as it orbits the Sun.
   - ❏ b. the weakness of the Sun as it ages.
   - ❏ c. the type of rays that the Sun gives off.

2. The imaginary line through Earth from the North Pole to the South Pole is called the
   - ❏ a. Pole line.
   - ❏ b. equator.
   - ❏ c. axis.

3. Direct light and heat warm the half of Earth
   - ❏ a. tilted toward the Sun.
   - ❏ b. tilted away from the Sun.
   - ❏ c. facing the Moon.

4. A region called _____ receives direct sunlight year-round and is always hot.
   - ❏ a. the North Pole
   - ❏ b. the South Pole
   - ❏ c. the tropics

5. The sharp angle between the Sun and the North Pole and South Pole causes them to be
   - ❏ a. hot all year.
   - ❏ b. cold all year.
   - ❏ c. hot in the summer and cold in the winter.

Understanding Ideas

6. The article suggests that in different regions of the world, seasons
   - ❏ a. are exactly alike.
   - ❏ b. are different.
   - ❏ c. often do not exist.

7. An example of a place that has a season of complete darkness and one of constant daylight is
   - ❏ a. the tropics.
   - ❏ b. the Sun.
   - ❏ c. the North Pole.

8. It is possible to conclude from the article that the season in the half of Earth tilted away from the Sun is
   - ❏ a. summer.
   - ❏ b. winter.
   - ❏ c. the dry season.

9. It is possible to infer from the article that when the northern half of Earth is tilted toward the Sun, the southern half is
   - ❏ a. tilted away from the Sun.
   - ❏ b. also tilted toward the Sun.
   - ❏ c. straight up and down.

10. It is possible to infer from the article that when it is summer in the northern half of Earth, it is _____ in the southern half.
    - ❏ a. summer
    - ❏ b. winter
    - ❏ c. the wet season

Repairing the Ozone Layer

The ozone layer is a layer of gas in the upper part of Earth's atmosphere. It is important to living things because it blocks harmful rays from the Sun. The ozone layer has changed because of people's use of some chemical gases found in spray cans and air conditioners. In some parts of the ozone layer, holes have formed. In other places, the layer has grown thin. As the layer becomes damaged, more of the Sun's detrimental rays reach Earth. Harmful waves from the Sun can cause skin cancer. These rays can also harm trees, crops, and sea creatures.

One way to study the ozone problem is from space. Astronaut Ellen Ochoa and others have studied changes in the ozone layer. They have measured the ozone layer and its holes. They have also measured harmful rays given off by the Sun.

These studies help scientists understand how the ozone layer might be repaired. The Sun can cause car exhaust on the ground to form ozone gas. On the ground, ozone harms life and forms smog. Scientists believe that ozone on the ground may someday join the ozone layer high in the sky. How this might happen or how long it might take is not yet fully understood. In the meantime, people can protect the ozone layer by not using chemicals that harm it.

1. **Recognizing Words in Context**

   Find the word *detrimental* in the passage. One definition below is closest to the meaning of that word. One definition has the opposite or nearly opposite meaning. The remaining definition has a completely different meaning. Label the definitions C for *closest*, O for *opposite or nearly opposite*, and D for *different*.

   _____ a. helpful

   _____ b. delaying

   _____ c. damaging

2. **Distinguishing Fact from Opinion**

   Two of the statements below present *facts*, which can be proved correct. The other statement is an *opinion*, which expresses someone's thoughts or beliefs. Label the statements F for *fact* and O for *opinion*.

   _____ a. The ozone problem is one of the most serious problems facing humans.

   _____ b. The ozone layer absorbs unsafe rays of sunlight.

   _____ c. Astronauts have studied the ozone layer.

3. **Keeping Events in Order**

Label the statements below 1, 2, and 3 to show the order in which the events happen.

_____ a. Scientists examine data gathered by astronauts to learn how the ozone layer might be repaired.

_____ b. Astronauts study the ozone layer and its holes.

_____ c. Chemical gases cause holes to form in the ozone.

4. **Making Correct Inferences**

Two of the statements below are correct *inferences,* or reasonable guesses. They are based on information in the passage. The other statement is an incorrect, or faulty, inference. Label the statements C for *correct* inference and F for *faulty* inference.

_____ a. There is something people can do to help protect the ozone layer.

_____ b. It doesn't matter if the ozone layer disappears because new ozone on the ground will join the ozone layer.

_____ c. As the ozone layer grows thin, there will be more cases of skin cancer and more harm done to forests, crops, and sea creatures.

5. **Understanding Main Ideas**

One of the statements below expresses the main idea of the passage. One statement is too general, or too broad. The other explains only part of the passage; it is too narrow. Label the statements M for *main idea*, B for *too broad,* and N for *too narrow.*

_____ a. Astronauts have studied the ozone problem from space.

_____ b. Damage to the ozone layer is creating hazardous conditions on Earth.

_____ c. The Sun can be helpful and harmful to life on Earth.

Correct Answers, Part A _____

Correct Answers, Part B _____

Total Correct Answers _____

Earthquakes

Earthquakes are movements in Earth's crust that cause the ground to shake. Earth's crust consists of its surface plus the rocky layer beneath it. Earthquakes can be slight tremors or fierce jolts. The force of large earthquakes causes great destruction. Buildings and homes collapse. Water, gas, and power lines are badly damaged. Landslides, as well as huge ocean waves called tsunamis, may be set in motion. Many lives are lost. Scientists study earthquakes in order to learn how to make better predictions about when and where future quakes may hit.

Earthquakes result from the movement of huge slabs of rock called plates. Gaps between these plates are called faults. The biggest faults lie between large plates. It is here that the strongest earthquakes occur. Quakes can occur all over the world, but most of them occur along large fault lines on both sides of the Pacific Ocean.

An earthquake starts deep below ground. As two plates grind slowly against each other, pressure builds up until suddenly the edges of the plates snap and the plates move more quickly. This jolt sends waves of energy through the earth. These waves—called shock waves—move up to the earth's surface, causing an earthquake.

Scientists measure the movements of the plates to learn more about earthquakes. A seismograph is a device that measures the ground's movements. Other meters, such as the strainmeter and tiltmeter, measure changes in Earth's crust. Lasers are used to detect small movements across fault lines. A scale called the Richter scale measures the force of an earthquake.

Scientists can learn about earthquakes, but they will be never be able to prevent earthquakes. Even though scientists today know much more about earthquakes than they did in the past, it is still difficult to predict earthquakes accurately. The best scientists can do is to warn people where quakes are likely to happen so that governments and other organizations can prepare.

Governments prepare for earthquakes by setting up training classes and creating strict building codes. Students in schools have earthquake drills. They learn to stand under doorframes or lie down under desks and tables during quakes. Building codes require that architects and construction companies create structures that can withstand strong shock waves. In some places, there are even power lines that can bend with the shock waves of a quake. For now, the best response to quakes is to be well prepared for them.

Reading Time _____

Recalling Facts

1. Movements in Earth's crust that cause the ground to shake are called
   - ❏ a. hurricanes.
   - ❏ b. tsunamis.
   - ❏ c. earthquakes.

2. Gaps in the rocky plates beneath Earth's surface are called
   - ❏ a. ridges.
   - ❏ b. faults.
   - ❏ c. swells.

3. A device scientists use to measure movements in the ground is a
   - ❏ a. barometer.
   - ❏ b. seismograph.
   - ❏ c. radiosonde.

4. What is one way that governments prepare for earthquakes?
   - ❏ a. They urge people to move somewhere else.
   - ❏ b. They require builders to follow strict codes.
   - ❏ c. They use explosives to eliminate pressure between plates.

5. The scale used to measure the force of an earthquake is the
   - ❏ a. pH scale.
   - ❏ b. balance scale.
   - ❏ c. Richter scale.

Understanding Ideas

6. From the article, you can infer that an earthquake would be most likely to occur in the
   - ❏ a. African nations along the Atlantic Ocean.
   - ❏ b. Asian nations along the Pacific Ocean.
   - ❏ c. European nations along the Baltic Sea.

7. It is possible to conclude from the article that scientists who wanted to examine vibrations along faults would use
   - ❏ a. building codes.
   - ❏ b. seismographs.
   - ❏ c. lasers.

8. The article suggests that predicting earthquakes
   - ❏ a. has become an exact science.
   - ❏ b. is difficult.
   - ❏ c. has never been done correctly.

9. The article suggests that preventing earthquakes from happening
   - ❏ a. is already possible.
   - ❏ b. will be possible someday.
   - ❏ c. will never be possible.

10. If an earthquake occurred in your area while you were in school, it would be wise for you to
    - ❏ a. get under your desk.
    - ❏ b. run for an exit door.
    - ❏ c. try to get out a window.

Not Aftershocks After All

A large earthquake is often followed by smaller quakes called aftershocks. In 1992, an earthquake in the Mojave Desert in southeastern California brought up new questions for scientists. For the first time, scientists were able to measure several earthquakes in the same region. The quakes that followed the first were large and distant. These quakes were not aftershocks: they were separate earthquakes. Could they have been caused or brought about in some way by the first desert quake?

To find out, scientists began to look for like patterns in data from other earthquakes. They found no similar events in their data. They began to look at reports that were made before the invention of the machines that measure earthquakes. One set of earthquakes that occurred in the midwestern United States in 1812 caught their eye. People living at that time told of strong "aftershocks." From the reported distance, motion, and size of these shocks, it seems doubtful that these shocks were really aftershocks. It is more likely that they were separate earthquakes triggered by the first quakes.

Like the recent desert quake, the quakes in 1812 seem to have caused other quakes. How this might happen is not yet known. Scientists continue to look at past accounts of earthquakes and to measure new quakes to find an answer.

1. **Recognizing Words in Context**

   Find the word *triggered* in the passage. One definition below is closest to the meaning of that word. One definition has the opposite or nearly opposite meaning. The remaining definition has a completely different meaning. Label the definitions C for *closest*, O for *opposite or nearly opposite*, and D for *different*.

   _____ a. increased

   _____ b. caused

   _____ c. prevented

2. **Distinguishing Fact from Opinion**

   Two of the statements below present *facts*, which can be proved correct. The other statement is an *opinion*, which expresses someone's thoughts or beliefs. Label the statements F for *fact* and O for *opinion*.

   _____ a. Large, distant quakes after the 1992 desert quake were not aftershocks.

   _____ b. People's descriptions of past earthquakes are the best source of information about quakes.

   _____ c. Aftershocks are small, nearby jolts that follow an earthquake.

3. Keeping Events in Order

Label the statements below 1, 2, and 3 to show the order in which the events happened.

_____ a. Scientists were surprised, so they looked for a similar pattern in data from other earthquakes.

_____ b. Scientists found accounts of earthquakes in 1812 that described similar events.

_____ c. The desert quake of 1992 was followed by large, distant quakes.

4. Making Correct Inferences

Two of the statements below are correct *inferences,* or reasonable guesses. They are based on information in the passage. The other statement is an incorrect, or faulty, inference. Label the statements C for *correct* inference and F for *faulty* inference.

_____ a. All jolts that follow a quake are really separate earthquakes.

_____ b. It is likely that an earthquake can bring about other earthquakes.

_____ c. Eyewitness accounts of earthquakes from long ago help scientists learn about earthquakes.

5. Understanding Main Ideas

One of the statements below expresses the main idea of the passage. One statement is too general, or too broad. The other explains only part of the passage; it is too narrow. Label the statements M for *main idea,* B for *too broad,* and N for *too narrow.*

_____ a. Scientists are trying to determine if one large earthquake can cause other large quakes.

_____ b. The earthquakes of 1812 were followed by some unusual jolts.

_____ c. An earthquake is a powerful event with many effects.

Correct Answers, Part A _____

Correct Answers, Part B _____

Total Correct Answers _____

Dinosaurs: All Shapes and Sizes

Dinosaurs came in all shapes and sizes. The structures of their bodies were related to their roles in the animal kingdom. Some ate plants, and some ate animals. The largest meat-eating dinosaur was the giganotosaurus. It had teeth more than 15 centimeters (6 inches) long. This beast was 13 meters (42 feet) long and weighed 8 tons. The size of its teeth and body made it a fierce attacker. Its teeth could easily shred the skin and bones of its prey.

Not all meat eaters were so large and fierce. The smallest meat-eating dinosaur was the compsognathus. It was about the size of a chicken, and it had a long tail. Another group of meat eaters called raptors depended on their speed to catch prey. They could reach speeds of about 65 kilometers per hour (40 miles per hour). One of the fastest raptors, the struthiomimus, was about the size of an ostrich. In contrast, the large utahraptor was 6 meters (20 feet) long. This beast had sharp claws on its hands and feet and fed on larger dinosaurs.

Many plant-eating dinosaurs were prey for meat eaters. Unlike the meat eaters, most plant eaters did not have sharp teeth or claws to protect themselves. The largest plant eaters had long necks to reach leaves and branches in tall trees. The sheer size of these long-necked creatures helped protect them from attack. The four-legged seismosaurus was as long as half a football field and weighed 40 tons. Smaller four-legged plant eaters had to defend themselves from the fierce meat eaters in other ways.

The plant-eating ankylosaurus was built like a tank. This dinosaur was covered in armorlike bony material and had a clublike structure on its tail. By swinging its clubbed tail, this dinosaur could crush the legs of an attacker. Some plant-eating dinosaurs, like the gastonia, had spikes on their bodies for defense. Others, like the triceratops, had horns on their heads and armor on their necks. The horns could reach more than 1 meter (3 feet) long.

Unlike these plant eaters with four legs, most plant eaters with two legs were easy prey for large meat eaters. They had few ways to protect themselves. Some stayed in herds to keep safe. Others had lightweight legs built for speed. They tried to outrun their enemies. Those plant-eating dinosaurs that were able to avoid their predators could live to be up to 200 years old.

Reading Time _____

Recalling Facts

1. A _____ was a meat-eating creature 13 meters long with teeth more than 15 centimeters long.
   - ❑ a. triceratops
   - ❑ b. giganotosaurus
   - ❑ c. saber-toothed tiger

2. To catch prey, dinosaurs called raptors depended on their
   - ❑ a. speed.
   - ❑ b. clublike tails.
   - ❑ c. intelligence.

3. To reach leaves high in trees, plant-eating dinosaurs had
   - ❑ a. long teeth.
   - ❑ b. sharp claws.
   - ❑ c. long necks.

4. Plant-eating dinosaurs had armor, spikes, clubs, and horns to
   - ❑ a. catch prey.
   - ❑ b. defend themselves.
   - ❑ c. become better hunters.

5. Two-legged plant eaters protected themselves from meat eaters by
   - ❑ a. staying in herds or running.
   - ❑ b. attacking meat eaters.
   - ❑ c. scaring meat eaters with spikes and horns.

Understanding Ideas

6. It is likely that plant-eating dinosaurs didn't have long teeth and sharp claws because they
   - ❑ a. did not need these tools to feed on plants.
   - ❑ b. did not need to defend themselves.
   - ❑ c. faced no danger.

7. The article suggests that although the gigantosaurus was huge, the _____ was even bigger.
   - ❑ a. compsognathus
   - ❑ b. seismosaurus
   - ❑ c. triceratops

8. A large dinosaur with a very long neck was likely to be a
   - ❑ a. meat eater.
   - ❑ b. plant eater.
   - ❑ c. raptor.

9. A dinosaur with long teeth and sharp claws was likely to be
   - ❑ a. an ancient lion.
   - ❑ b. a plant eater.
   - ❑ c. a meat eater.

10. Which of the following would be the least likely way that plant-eating dinosaurs would have protected themselves?
   - ❑ a. by using long, sharp teeth to bite attackers
   - ❑ b. by outrunning attackers
   - ❑ c. by swinging weaponlike tails at attackers

22 B Are Birds Related to Dinosaurs?

Believe it or not, dinosaurs had a lot in common with modern birds. Similar to the tyrannosaurus, birds walk on two legs, have claws on their scaly feet, and lay eggs. Birds have even more in common with some other dinosaurs. Fossils show that some dinosaurs had feathers. Instead of collarbones, some had wishbones, as birds do. In general, the bones and the skeletons of birds are a lot like those of the dinosaurs.

Indeed, some birds appear to be related to dinosaurs. Some scientists think there were dinosaurs that did not die out but instead evolved into birds over time. Fossils of creatures with traits of both birds and dinosaurs show how this may have happened.

A dinosaur called archaeopteryx had feathers like a bird. It may have been able to fly too. Unlike a bird, this creature had teeth, clawed wings, and a long, bony tail. In this way, it resembled a dinosaur. A few years ago, scientist Cathy Forster found a similar fossil. This creature, called rahonavis, had feathers, clawed wings, and a long, bony tail. Fossils of these creatures and other feathered dinosaurs suggest that birds may in fact be living dinosaurs. There is still much research to be done in this area, however, and many scientists still believe dinosaurs are most closely related to modern reptiles.

1. **Recognizing Words in Context**

   Find the word *resembled* in the passage. One definition below is closest to the meaning of that word. One definition has the opposite or nearly opposite meaning. The remaining definition has a completely different meaning. Label the definitions C for *closest*, O for *opposite or nearly opposite*, and D for *different*.

   _____ a. looked like

   _____ b. mixed

   _____ c. differed from

2. **Distinguishing Fact from Opinion**

   Two of the statements below present *facts*, which can be proved correct. The other statement is an *opinion*, which expresses someone's thought or belief. Label the statements F for *fact* and O for *opinion*.

   _____ a. The evidence that birds are living dinosaurs is weak.

   _____ b. Birds and dinosaurs share some common traits.

   _____ c. Some dinosaurs had feathers.

3. Keeping Events in Order

Two of the statements below describe events that happened at the same time. The other statement describes an event that happened before or after those events. Label them S for *same time*, B for *before*, and A for *after*.

_____ a. There were creatures with feathers, clawed wings, and long, bony tails.

_____ b. A bird without teeth or a long tail flew in the sky.

_____ c. The fierce tyrannosaurus walked the earth.

4. Making Correct Inferences

Two of the statements below are correct *inferences*, or reasonable guesses. They are based on information in the passage. The other statement is an incorrect, or faulty, inference. Label the statements C for *correct* inference and F for *faulty* inference.

_____ a. Dinosaurs were more like birds than like mammals.

_____ b. The wisest scientists believe dinosaurs developed into modern birds.

_____ c. Some dinosaurs may have been able to fly.

5. Understanding Main Ideas

One of the statements below expresses the main idea of the passage. One statement is too general, or too broad. The other explains only part of the passage; it is too narrow. Label the statements M for *main idea*, B for *too broad*, and N for *too narrow*.

_____ a. Dinosaurs of all shapes and sizes roamed the earth at one time.

_____ b. Some dinosaurs had feathers and may have been able to fly.

_____ c. Some scientists believe that dinosaurs are the ancestors of modern birds.

Correct Answers, Part A _____

Correct Answers, Part B _____

Total Correct Answers _____

When you hear energy mentioned on the evening news, the information usually concerns fuels or electricity. In the branch of science called physics, however, energy refers to the ability to move an object. Without energy, there would be no motion in the universe. Physics helps explain the relationship between energy and objects.

There are several kinds of energy. Two important types are kinetic energy and potential energy; they are key concepts in physics. A moving object has a type of energy called kinetic energy. In contrast, an object has potential energy, or stored energy, when it is not moving but is in a position to move. Good examples of kinetic and potential energy can be found at a playground.

A child uses kinetic energy to move up the steps of a slide. When the child reaches the top of the slide, the kinetic energy has turned into potential energy. From this raised position, the child can use the potential energy to slide down again. The potential energy of the child changes back to kinetic energy as he or she begins to move down the slide.

A child on a swing shows kinetic and potential energy too. The motion of the swing as it goes up and then back down is kinetic energy. When the swing reaches its top height, it stops for an instant. At this instant of rest in the raised position, the swing has potential energy. As the swing starts to move back down, the potential energy starts to change back to kinetic energy.

In physics, energy is never created or destroyed. It just changes from one form to another or passes from one object to another. When a bat strikes a pitched baseball, the kinetic energy of the moving bat changes the direction of the ball. The energy of the bat is not lost; it is passed on to the ball. The ball then flies through the air until it is caught or until it hits the ground, rolls, and then stops.

A ball slows down as it rolls along the ground because of friction. As molecules of the ball rub against molecules of the ground, kinetic energy changes to heat energy. When the ball stops, it no longer has energy, but the energy has not been lost. It has only changed its form because of friction. As soon as a person picks the ball up, it will once again have energy.

Reading Time _____

Recalling Facts

1. The kind of energy a moving object has is called
   - ❏ a. potential energy.
   - ❏ b. kinetic energy.
   - ❏ c. gravity.

2. An object that has stored energy when it is at rest in a raised position has
   - ❏ a. potential energy.
   - ❏ b. friction.
   - ❏ c. kinetic energy.

3. A child sitting at the top of a slide has
   - ❏ a. potential energy.
   - ❏ b. solar energy.
   - ❏ c. mechanical energy.

4. Energy is never
   - ❏ a. changed from one form to another.
   - ❏ b. passed on to another object.
   - ❏ c. created or destroyed.

5. The rubbing action that changes kinetic energy to heat energy is called
   - ❏ a. gravity.
   - ❏ b. friction.
   - ❏ c. mass.

Understanding Ideas

6. From the information in the article, you can infer that an ice skater doing a jump has
   - ❏ a. potential energy.
   - ❏ b. kinetic energy.
   - ❏ c. solar energy.

7. It is possible to conclude from the article that snowboarders have potential energy when they are
   - ❏ a. flying into the air.
   - ❏ b. standing at the top of a hill.
   - ❏ c. lying on their backs at the bottom of a hill after wiping out.

8. The article suggests that when a bat strikes a baseball, the energy from the moving bat is
   - ❏ a. destroyed.
   - ❏ b. passed on to the ball.
   - ❏ c. lost forever.

9. The article suggests that one form of energy
   - ❏ a. cannot change to another form of energy.
   - ❏ b. can change another form of energy into a solid object.
   - ❏ c. can change to another form of energy.

10. It is possible to conclude from the article that an object cannot move without
    - ❏ a. friction.
    - ❏ b. energy.
    - ❏ c. gravity.

23 B   The Science of Kickball

Keith was having trouble concentrating in science class. Gym class was next. Keith wanted to stop thinking about energy and start using a little of his own energy. As the bell rang, the science teacher, Mrs. Pham, assigned homework. The students were supposed to write about a situation in which they experienced kinetic and potential energy.

When it was Keith's turn at the plate in the kickball game, he wanted to focus on kicking the ball over the outfielders' heads. Instead, all he could think about was the homework for science class. As the ball rolled toward him, Keith thought, "An object in motion has kinetic energy." Keith's foot struck the ball and sent it high into the air. Keith thought, "The kinetic energy from my moving foot went into the ball, changing the way it was going."

As Keith ran toward first base, the ball reached its highest point in the air and seemed to hesitate for an instant. Keith knew that at this raised point of rest, the ball had potential energy. As soon as the ball began to fall, the potential energy changed to kinetic energy. Just as Keith got to first base, one of his classmates caught the ball before it hit the ground. Keith was out, but at least his homework was almost done.

1. **Recognizing Words in Context**

   Find the word *hesitate* in the passage. One definition below is closest to the meaning of that word. One definition has the opposite or nearly opposite meaning. The remaining definition has a completely different meaning. Label the definitions C for *closest*, O for *opposite or nearly opposite*, and D for *different*.

   _____ a. fly

   _____ b. continue

   _____ c. pause

2. **Distinguishing Fact from Opinion**

   Two of the statements below present *facts*, which can be proved correct. The other statement is an *opinion*, which expresses someone's thoughts or beliefs. Label the statements F for *fact* and O for *opinion*.

   _____ a. An object in motion has kinetic energy.

   _____ b. Gym class is more fun than science class.

   _____ c. A ball at a raised point of rest has potential energy.

3. Keeping Events in Order

Label the statements below 1, 2, and 3 to show the order in which the events happen.

_____ a. The ball reaches its highest point and is at rest for an instant.

_____ b. The kinetic energy from the kick of Keith's foot changes the direction of the ball.

_____ c. The ball falls and is caught by a classmate.

4. Making Correct Inferences

Two of the statements below are correct *inferences,* or reasonable guesses. They are based on information in the passage. The other statement is an incorrect, or faulty, inference. Label the statements C for *correct* inference and F for *faulty* inference.

_____ a. After Keith lifted back his leg to kick the ball, his leg had potential energy.

_____ b. As the ball flew upward into the air, it had kinetic energy.

_____ c. Running to first base is an example of potential energy.

5. Understanding Main Ideas

One of the statements below expresses the main idea of the passage. One statement is too general, or too broad. The other explains only part of the passage; it is too narrow. Label the statements M for *main idea*, B for *too broad*, and N for *too narrow*.

_____ a. Different forms of energy are a part of daily life.

_____ b. A kickball game can provide examples of kinetic energy and potential energy.

_____ c. When the ball began to fall out of the air, potential energy changed to kinetic energy.

Correct Answers, Part A _____

Correct Answers, Part B _____

Total Correct Answers _____

People and animals share certain characteristics. It is common to hear someone compare a person to a lone wolf or a wise owl. A finicky person is said to eat like a bird, and a determined person is said to be as stubborn as a mule. These sayings do not necessarily give an accurate picture of the animals they describe, however. Animals, like humans, are complex creatures, and while they may act particular ways in certain situations, their behaviors may be much different at other times.

The reputation of a mule as being a stubborn animal is not entirely fair. True, a mule will usually refuse to cooperate with a person it does not know or trust; it may even be downright hostile. But mules can be of great service to people. Farmers say that once a mule's trust is gained, the mule will do almost any task its owner requires. The mule's intelligence and strength have made this animal a superb worker for thousands of years.

A person who prefers to work or live alone may be described as a lone wolf. Real wolves, however, usually live in packs. It is easier for them to hunt their favorite prey—deer and moose—when they work together as a group. Occasionally a young adult wolf will leave a pack and live by itself for a while before it joins or starts another pack.

Calling an intelligent person "as wise as an owl" is not really a compliment. Owls have very large eyes for hunting. The all-knowing gaze of these huge eyes gives an owl a look of wisdom. For a bird of its size, however, the owl has only average intelligence. The owl's most remarkable trait is its keen vision. Its eyes function like binoculars and are especially effective in limited light.

Birds do not seem to eat much only because they are small, lightweight animals. They have thin, hollow bones and air sacs like balloons throughout their bodies. In relation to its body weight, however, a bird eats quite a bit because it needs a lot of energy for flying. If a bird were the size of a human, it would need to eat 150 bananas a day to meet its energy requirements!

The next time someone uses a phrase that contains a description of an animal, remember that things are not always as they appear. Find out the facts to learn the true habits of animals.

Reading Time _____

Recalling Facts

1. A person who is a picky eater is said to eat like a
   - ❑ a. horse.
   - ❑ b. hog.
   - ❑ c. bird.

2. A mule is
   - ❑ a. an animal too stubborn to use for work.
   - ❑ b. an animal that is no longer used by farmers anywhere.
   - ❑ c. a superb work animal for people it trusts.

3. A wolf is an animal that
   - ❑ a. usually lives alone.
   - ❑ b. usually lives and hunts in packs.
   - ❑ c. eats every hour.

4. In order to fly, birds
   - ❑ a. have thin, hollow bones.
   - ❑ b. eat twice a day.
   - ❑ c. rarely eat.

5. A common myth about owls is that they
   - ❑ a. eat very little.
   - ❑ b. make good pets.
   - ❑ c. are exceptionally wise.

Understanding Ideas

6. People believe that mules are stubborn and wolves are solitary because of
   - ❑ a. the way they always act.
   - ❑ b. the way they act occasionally.
   - ❑ c. actions that have never been seen.

7. The article suggests that people form ideas about animals
   - ❑ a. by watching their actions.
   - ❑ b. without knowing what they look like.
   - ❑ c. from the way animals are described in common phrases.

8. In addition to the effort needed to fly, what is another likely reason that birds eat so many times during the day?
   - ❑ a. They rarely stop moving and need lots of energy.
   - ❑ b. They eat only two or three seeds for an average meal.
   - ❑ c. They have to gain a lot of weight because they hibernate for half the year.

9. Why might some phrases about animals remain common even though they are not really accurate?
   - ❑ a. People like to ignore the truth.
   - ❑ b. Most people have not studied animals in detail.
   - ❑ c. People don't give any thought to what they say.

10. Mules have been used as work animals for thousands of years, and so you can conclude that mules are
    - ❑ a. almost as smart as people.
    - ❑ b. faster than machines.
    - ❑ c. not always stubborn.

24 B   An Unusual Bird and Its Unforgettable Food

The Clark's nutcracker is a bird that lives in the mountains of western North America. As fall nears, the nutcracker begins to collect and store pine seeds, also called pine nuts. First, the bird picks up the seeds and holds them in a pouch under its tongue. One bird can carry 90 of these seeds at once. Next, the nutcracker stores the seeds in small holes in the ground. Between August and December each year, a nutcracker will store up to 33,000 pine seeds. The nutcracker hides the seeds in as many as 2,500 holes.

Clark's nutcrackers raise their young in the early spring. It is hard to find food at this time because there is still much snow in the mountains. To feed its young, the nutcracker must find the seeds it stored in the fall. First the nutcracker looks for landmarks to remember where it buried seeds. A landmark might be a certain tree or boulder. Then the nutcracker uses the distance from landmarks to find the stored seeds. Finally, the nutcracker carries the seeds back to the nest to feed the hungry chicks. In the end, an adult nutcracker returns to hundreds of sites to retrieve stored seeds. The nutcracker's memory is put to the test, and its food proves to be unforgettable.

1. **Recognizing Words in Context**

   Find the word *retrieve* in the passage. One definition below is closest to the meaning of that word. One definition has the opposite or nearly opposite meaning. The remaining definition has a completely different meaning. Label the definitions C for *closest*, O for *opposite or nearly opposite*, and D for *different*.

   _____ a. fetch

   _____ b. eat

   _____ c. lose

2. **Distinguishing Fact from Opinion**

   Two of the statements below present *facts*, which can be proved correct. The other statement is an *opinion*, which expresses someone's thoughts or beliefs. Label the statements F for *fact* and O for *opinion*.

   _____ a. Nutcrackers use landmarks to find stored seeds.

   _____ b. Nutcrackers depend on their stored seeds for survival.

   _____ c. The nutcracker is an amazing bird.

3. Keeping Events in Order

Label the statements below 1, 2, and 3 to show the order in which the events happen.

_____ a. Nutcracker chicks hatch.

_____ b. Nutcrackers find their stored seeds to feed their young.

_____ c. Nutcrackers store seeds in holes in the ground.

4. Making Correct Inferences

Two of the statements below are correct *inferences*, or reasonable guesses. They are based on information in the passage. The other statement is an incorrect, or faulty, inference. Label the statements C for *correct* inference and F for *faulty* inference.

_____ a. Nutcracker chicks need to eat lots of pine seeds to be healthy.

_____ b. No other animal has a memory as good as the nutcracker's.

_____ c. Nutcrackers spend most of the fall gathering and storing seeds.

5. Understanding Main Ideas

One of the statements below expresses the main idea of the passage. One statement is too general, or too broad. The other explains only part of the passage; it is too narrow. Label the statements M for *main idea*, B for *too broad*, and N for *too narrow*.

_____ a. The Clark's nutcracker is able to remember hundreds of places where it has buried seeds.

_____ b. A pouch under its tongue allows a nutcracker to carry many seeds at once.

_____ c. Birds have different ways to survive the winter.

Correct Answers, Part A _____

Correct Answers, Part B _____

Total Correct Answers _____

Life Cycles of Wildflowers

A wildflower is a flowering plant that grows in the wild. Like other flowering plants, wildflowers have seeds that form in flowers when grains of pollen join with eggs found at the base of the petals. Wind and insects help transport pollen to the eggs.

The life cycles of wildflowers vary. Some wildflowers live short lives and grow flowers just once. Others live for many years and flower many times. All flowers, including wildflowers, are referred to as annuals, biennials, or perennials, depending on the length and pattern of the plant's life.

Texas bluebonnet, daisy fleabane, and Indian paintbrush are examples of annual wildflowers. Annual plants grow, flower, and produce seeds in a year or less. Summer annuals grow in the springtime. They flower by fall. The seeds of winter annuals grow into plants in the fall. The plants live through the winter and flower in the spring. Annuals die as soon as their flowers form seeds.

Annual wildflowers often grow in places where few other plants can survive all year. For part of the year, the climate in these places may be too harsh. The wildflowers survive these harsh seasons as seeds. Seeds can survive harsh conditions that plants cannot. It is hard for annuals to grow among plants that live for many years. With their short lives, they often cannot compete for space in the sun and soil. Annual wildflowers often can be seen alongside roads and in cleared lots.

Wildflowers that live for two growing seasons are called biennials. Desert marigolds and some types of black-eyed Susans are examples of biennials. During the first growing season, this kind of wildflower grows and gathers strength. It takes in energy from the sun to make food that is stored in a thick root called a taproot. The second growing season begins after winter. Before the second growing season ends, a biennial plant flowers and forms seeds. The plant dies after seeds are formed.

Many wildflowers are perennials that can live for years and years. Examples are dandelions and violets. Some of these plants flower every year. They produce many seeds in their lives. Others, like the water lily, grow for a few years before they flower and produce seeds. Perennial plants depend on their roots to live through cold winters. The roots stay alive when the rest of the plant dies. In spring, new stems, leaves, and flowers grow from the roots.

Reading Time _____

Recalling Facts

1. Perennial plants live for
   - ❏ a. less than one year.
   - ❏ b. two growing seasons.
   - ❏ c. many years.

2. Seeds form in
   - ❏ a. flowers.
   - ❏ b. leaves.
   - ❏ c. roots.

3. An annual wildflower most often grows in
   - ❏ a. open spaces.
   - ❏ b. shaded spaces.
   - ❏ c. crowded spaces.

4. A biennial wildflower dies
   - ❏ a. before it forms seeds.
   - ❏ b. after it forms seeds.
   - ❏ c. within one year.

5. Winter annuals live through the winter and flower in the
   - ❏ a. winter.
   - ❏ b. spring.
   - ❏ c. fall.

Understanding Ideas

6. It is possible to conclude from the article that wildflowers grow
   - ❏ a. only in the summer.
   - ❏ b. only in the spring and fall.
   - ❏ c. in every season of the year.

7. The article suggests that if a wildflower did not grow flowers,
   - ❏ a. seeds would still be formed.
   - ❏ b. no seeds would be formed.
   - ❏ c. seeds would be formed only in good weather.

8. The article suggests that during harsh seasons, wildflowers
   - ❏ a. survive as seeds or roots.
   - ❏ b. die out.
   - ❏ c. grow quickly.

9. It is likely that annual wildflowers would grow well
   - ❏ a. in thick jungles.
   - ❏ b. in deserts that get occasional rain.
   - ❏ c. among perennial wildflowers.

10. If a plant in the wild has no visible flowers in the spring, it
    - ❏ a. cannot be a wildflower.
    - ❏ b. must be dead.
    - ❏ c. could be a summer annual.

Searching for Desert Wildflowers

Linda had not gone looking for wildflowers with Aunt Clara since the previous spring. Aunt Clara studied plants for the Desert Research Center. Every year, Aunt Clara asked Linda to help her with her work. As they drove out of town, Linda remembered the field of Mexican goldpoppies they had studied last time. The wildflowers had looked like a soft orange blanket covering the desert.

Soon Aunt Clara pulled the car off the road. Linda scanned the desert for the golden flowers but saw only pale green cacti.

Confused, Linda asked her aunt, "Where are all the poppies?"

"Poppy seeds didn't grow this year. The seeds are waiting underground for better conditions. The seeds can wait 10 or more years before they grow." Aunt Clara explained that the goldpoppy seeds grew only if they had received enough rain in September and October. Even with plenty of rain, seeds might not grow. Temperature and the amount of sunlight were also important.

If the conditions were good in early fall, the wildflower seeds would slowly grow into small plants. As the ground heated in March and April, flower stalks would shoot up. The flowers would live only long enough to deposit new seeds in the soil.

As they walked, Linda thought of all the dormant goldpoppy seeds below her feet. They were waiting for just the right conditions to grow.

1. **Recognizing Words in Context**

   Find the word *dormant* in the passage. One definition below is closest to the meaning of that word. One definition has the opposite or nearly opposite meaning. The remaining definition has a completely different meaning. Label the definitions C for *closest,* O for *opposite or nearly opposite,* and D for *different.*

   _____ a. active

   _____ b. inactive

   _____ c. actual

2. **Distinguishing Fact from Opinion**

   Two of the statements below present *facts,* which can be proved correct. The other statement is an *opinion,* which expresses someone's thoughts or beliefs. Label the statements F for *fact* and O for *opinion.*

   _____ a. A field of poppies looks like a soft blanket.

   _____ b. Seeds can wait underground for many years before they grow.

   _____ c. Rain in September and October can cause Mexican goldpoppy seeds to grow.

111

3. **Keeping Events in Order**

Label the statements below 1, 2, and 3 to show the order in which the events happen.

_____ a. Linda sees only pale green cacti.

_____ b. Aunt Clara explains why poppies didn't grow.

_____ c. Aunt Clara invites Linda to look for wildflowers.

4. **Making Correct Inferences**

Two of the statements below are correct *inferences,* or reasonable guesses. They are based on information in the passage. The other statement is an incorrect, or faulty, inference. Label the statements C for *correct* inference and F for *faulty* inference.

_____ a. Some desert wildflowers grow only when conditions are right.

_____ b. The poppy seeds will sprout if there is the right amount of sunlight.

_____ c. Desert wildflowers do not grow every year.

5. **Understanding Main Ideas**

One of the statements below expresses the main idea of the passage. One statement is too general, or too broad. The other explains only part of the passage; it is too narrow. Label the statements M for *main idea,* B for *too broad,* and N for *too narrow.*

_____ a. Wildflower seeds will not sprout unless a certain set of conditions is met.

_____ b. Mexican goldpoppy seeds may not sprout for many years.

_____ c. Wildflowers can grow in harsh environments, such as deserts.

Correct Answers, Part A _____

Correct Answers, Part B _____

Total Correct Answers _____

Answer Key

Reading Rate Graph

Comprehension Score Graph

Comprehension Skills Profile Graph

ANSWER KEY

1A   1. b   2. c   3. b   4. a   5. c   6. b   7. a   8. c   9. a   10. c

1B   1. D, C, O   2. F, O, F   3. S, A, S   4. C, C, F   5. B, M, N

2A   1. a   2. b   3. b   4. c   5. a   6. c   7. b   8. a   9. b   10. c

2B   1. O, C, D   2. O, F, F   3. 2, 3, 1   4. F, C, C   5. N, B, M

3A   1. c   2. b   3. a   4. a   5. c   6. b   7. a   8. c   9. c   10. a

3B   1. D, O, C   2. O, F, F   3. 1, 3, 2   4. C, C, F   5. B, M, N

4A   1. b   2. c   3. b   4. c   5. a   6. c   7. b   8. a   9. a   10. c

4B   1. D, O, C   2. F, O, F   3. 1, 2, 3   4. F, C, C   5. M, B, N

5A   1. a   2. b   3. a   4. c   5. c   6. b   7. c   8. a   9. a   10. c

5B   1. O, C, D   2. O, F, F   3. 2, 3, 1   4. C, F, C   5. N, M, B

6A   1. b   2. b   3. a   4. a   5. c   6. c   7. b   8. b   9. a   10. c

6B   1. C, D, O   2. F, F, O   3. 1, 3, 2   4. F, C, C   5. N, M, B

7A   1. a   2. b   3. b   4. c   5. c   6. a   7. c   8. b   9. b   10. a

7B   1. D, C, O   2. F, O, F   3. 2, 1, 3   4. F, C, C   5. N, B, M

8A   1. a   2. c   3. c   4. a   5. b   6. c   7. a   8. c   9. b   10. c

8B   1. D, O, C   2. O, F, F   3. 1, 2, 3   4. C, F, C   5. B, N, M

9A   1. b   2. c   3. a   4. c   5. c   6. c   7. a   8. a   9. b   10. a

9B   1. C, O, D   2. F, F, O   3. 3, 1, 2   4. C, C, F   5. B, N, M

10A   1. a   2. c   3. a   4. c   5. c   6. c   7. b   8. a   9. a   10. b

10B   1. D, O, C   2. F, O, F   3. 2, 1, 3   4. F, C, C   5. N, B, M

11A   1. b   2. a   3. c   4. b   5. a   6. b   7. c   8. a   9. b   10. c

11B   1. O, C, D   2. O, F, F   3. 3, 1, 2   4. C, F, C   5. N, M, B

12A   1. a   2. b   3. b   4. c   5. b   6. a   7. c   8. b   9. a   10. c

12B   1. O, C, D   2. F, O, F   3. 1, 3, 2   4. C, C, F   5. M, B, N

13A   1. a   2. c   3. b   4. c   5. c   6. c   7. b   8. a   9. a   10. c

13B   1. O, C, D   2. F, O, F   3. 2, 3, 1   4. F, C, C   5. N, M, B

14A	1. c	2. a	3. b	4. a	5. c	6. b	7. c	8. a	9. a	10. b
14B	1. C, D, O	2. F, O, F	3. 2, 1, 3	4. F, C, C	5. B, N, M
15A	1. b	2. a	3. c	4. b	5. a	6. b	7. a	8. c	9. b	10. a
15B	1. C, D, O	2. F, F, O	3. 1, 3, 2	4. C, C, F	5. B, N, M
16A	1. c	2. c	3. a	4. c	5. a	6. a	7. c	8. a	9. a	10. b
16B	1. O, D, C	2. O, F, F	3. 3, 2, 1	4. C, F, C	5. M, B, N
17A	1. b	2. a	3. c	4. c	5. c	6. a	7. b	8. c	9. b	10. a
17B	1. O, D, C	2. O, F, F	3. S, A, S	4. F, C, C	5. B, N, M
18A	1. a	2. c	3. b	4. a	5. b	6. c	7. a	8. c	9. b	10. b
18B	1. C, O, D	2. F, F, O	3. 2, 3, 1	4. C, C, F	5. B, M, N
19A	1. c	2. a	3. b	4. c	5. a	6. c	7. b	8. c	9. b	10. a
19B	1. C, O, D	2. F, F, O	3. 3, 1, 2	4. C, F, C	5. M, N, B
20A	1. a	2. c	3. a	4. c	5. b	6. b	7. c	8. b	9. a	10. b
20B	1. O, D, C	2. O, F, F	3. 3, 2, 1	4. C, F, C	5. N, M, B
21A	1. c	2. b	3. b	4. b	5. c	6. b	7. b	8. b	9. c	10. a
21B	1. D, C, O	2. F, O, F	3. 2, 3, 1	4. F, C, C	5. M, N, B
22A	1. b	2. a	3. c	4. b	5. a	6. a	7. b	8. b	9. c	10. a
22B	1. C, D, O	2. O, F, F	3. S, A, S	4. C, F, C	5. B, N, M
23A	1. b	2. a	3. a	4. c	5. b	6. b	7. b	8. b	9. c	10. b
23B	1. D, O, C	2. F, O, F	3. 2, 1, 3	4. C, C, F	5. B, M, N
24A	1. c	2. c	3. b	4. a	5. c	6. b	7. c	8. a	9. b	10. c
24B	1. C, D, O	2. F, F, O	3. 2, 3, 1	4. C, F, C	5. M, N, B
25A	1. c	2. a	3. a	4. b	5. b	6. c	7. b	8. a	9. b	10. c
25B	1. O, C, D	2. O, F, F	3. 2, 3, 1	4. C, F, C	5. M, N, B

READING RATE

Put an X on the line above each lesson number to show your reading time and words-per-minute rate for that lesson.

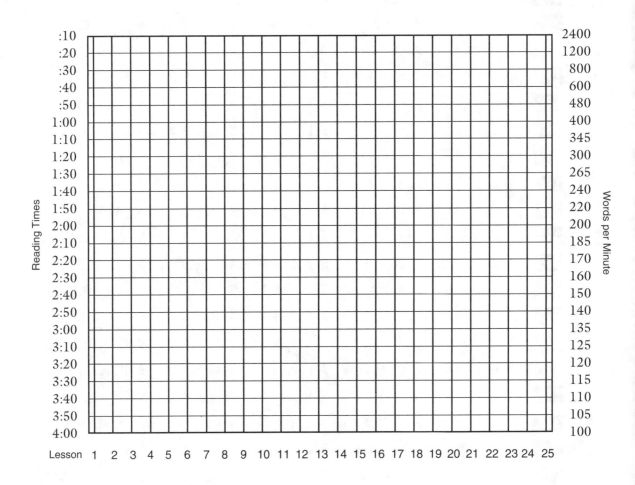

COMPREHENSION SCORE

Put an X on the line above each lesson number to indicate your total correct answers and comprehension score for that lesson.

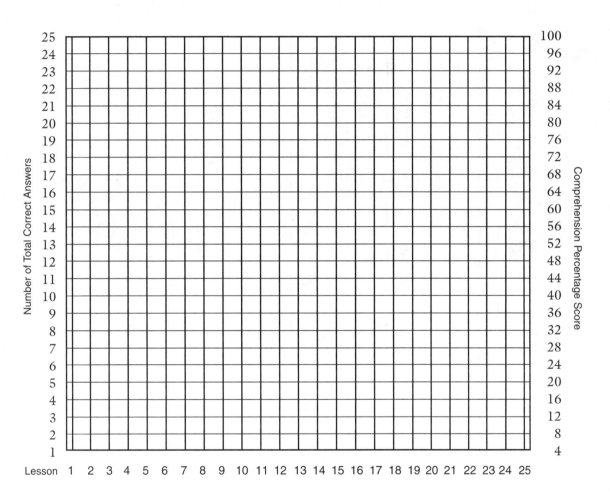

COMPREHENSION SKILLS PROFILE

Put an X in the box above each question type to indicate an incorrect reponse to any part of that question.

	Recognizing Words in Context	Distinguishing Fact from Opinion	Keeping Events in Order	Making Correct Inferences	Understanding Main Ideas
Lesson 1					
2					
3					
4					
5					
6					
7					
8					
9					
10					
11					
12					
13					
14					
15					
16					
17					
18					
19					
20					
21					
22					
23					
24					
25					